KT-449-580

Perspectives in English Book Three

Ray Beecroft & Graham Sanderson

St. Columba's High School,
Dunfermline.

Hart-Davis Educational

© 1983 Ray Beecroft and Graham Sanderson

ISBN 0 247 13165 2

Published by Hart-Davis Educational Ltd
a division of Granada Publishing
Frogmore, St Albans, Hertfordshire

Granada ®
Granada Publishing ®

All rights reserved. No part of this publication may be
reproduced, stored in a retrieval system, or transmitted, in
any form or by any means, electronic, mechanical, photocopying,
recording or otherwise, without prior permission of the
publishers.

Filmset and printed in Great Britain by
BAS Printers Limited, Over Wallop, Hampshire

Design and Cover Design : Ken Vail
Drawings
Robert Geary *pages* 62, 64, 71, 89, 91, 124, 141, 146, 148, 159, 161
Tony Morris *pages* 10, 116, 179, 180, 202
Barry Wilkinson *pages* 17, 72, 73, 75, 107, 128, 177, 197

Photographs
Popperfoto page 6; South African Tourist Corporation page 12; 'Fall of the
House of Usher' by Douglas Percy Bliss from *History of British Wood
Engraving* by Albert Garrett, Midas Books page 20; 'The Scream' by Edvard
Munch, Nasjonalgalleriet, Oslo page 21; Heather Angel pages 22, 100; Richard
and Sally Greenhill pages 26, 48, 156 (bottom left); Henry Grant pages 32, 40,
204; BBC Hulton Picture Library pages 44, 45, 102, 114; Barnaby's Picture
Library pages 53, 56, 57, (left), 58, 155 (top right, bottom left), 156 (top right,
middle left), 189, 210; John Topham Picture Library pages 55, 122, 154
(bottom), 155 (bottom right), 169, 192 (bottom), 211; Camera Press Ltd pages
57 (right) L. Smillie, 111 Norman Sklarewitz, 138 Colin Davey, 163 Valerie
Wilmer, 165, 167; Mary Evans Picture Library/Harry Price Collection,
University of London page 79; page 85 by permission of the British Library;
The Imperial War Museum page 86; Frank Lane Agency, Arthur Christiansen
page 92; Lowie Museum of Anthropology, University of California, Berkeley
pages 94–5; Health Education Council pages 112–3; the Tayside Health
Education Centre page 113, Sue Chapman page 118; Aerofilms Ltd page 150;
J Allan Cash Ltd pages 154 (top), 155 (top left), 156 (top left); Thomson
Holidays page 156 (middle right); Trusthouse Forte plc page 156 (bottom
right); Peter Mitchell page 174; Wiener Library Ltd and Zydowski Instytut
Historyczny, Warsaw page 192 (top); Wiener Library and 'The Yorkshire
Post' page 214.

Contents

To the Teacher

This book in the series aims to provide stimulating material appropriate to the ages and abilities of thirteen to fourteen-year-olds in a comprehensive school.

Nine of the chapters in Book Three are based on themes and contain material for discussion, comprehension and writing. There are also two Language chapters and a list of spelling groups. In addition, each thematic chapter is supplemented by a *Starting Point*, not related to the theme.

The thematic chapters are based on the assumption that much classroom work will involve discussion as well as writing. Questions and assignments in the text are identified by asterisks or by numbers. An asterisk denotes a question intended primarily for discussion; a numbered question usually demands a written response. These marks are for the teacher's convenience and are not intended to be prescriptive. Each thematic chapter also contains *A Closer Look*. This is a series of questions designed to explore a writer's technique or vocabulary in detail.

Specific language instruction in the book is grouped separately from the thematic chapters for ease of reference. A short index to language topics covered here and elsewhere in the book is given on page 223 .

The *Starting Points* offer stimulus for imaginative work; or attempt to teach a skill; or deal with a particular aspect of language.

G.S.
C.R.B.

PANIC

In the Box

Jonathan, the son of wealthy parents, has been kidnapped. He has been efficiently blindfolded and forced into a vehicle.

Jonathan found it difficult to gather anything about the changing of vehicles. They changed to what he thought must be another van, only a quiet, more expensive-sounding one. The transfer seemed to take place in a large garage, by the smell, and quite a lot of gear, including the tent-like bundles, was packed into the new vehicle. They set off again, the boss-man, John driving. He drove fast.

'We're not going to have a lot of time to spare,' he remarked. 'It's gone half past five already.'

'The start's at half six.'

'That's what I mean. By the time we get everything sorted out – and the lad here packed up.'

Jonathan could not work this out, and decided that he didn't like the prospect of being 'packed up'.

'What do you mean – packed up?' he asked.

Jamie's voice close beside him said, soothingly, 'It won't be for long, just to get you out without anybody seeing.'

To Jonathan this sounded hopeful, indicating that he might stand a chance of attracting attention if there were to be other people about, but optimism was instantly crushed by the driver saying, cuttingly, 'You don't have to answer *all* his questions, Jamie, for God's sake – the less he knows the better. You can start getting him fixed up now – we'll be there in ten minutes and we don't want to mess about. Everything else is ready to chuck out.'

'Who's got the transistor?' someone asked.

'I have. We're going to time it nicely for the weather forecast. Keep it turned up loud and that'll drown out any possible protests.'

'But we're going to gag him surely – ?'

'Cripes, yes! But we can't be too careful. Just like the dress rehearsal.'

It was all quite different suddenly, the real thing, the niceties dropped. Jonathan, instinctively uncooperative, out of plain funk, had no more chance to wonder what it was all about, was seized by a lot of rough hands and thrust uncompromisingly into some sort of a box, and a very small box at that, so that as he knelt, and was forced down by the back of his neck till his forehead touched his knees, the sides of the box were pressed against him on all sides, and when they put the lid down it was hard against his back and chained hands.

'Just trying it for size,' somebody said, and let him come upright again. Jonathan, no longer calm, but claustrophobically panic-stricken at the thought of being contained in such a tiny space, started to scream and struggle with such force that it took the three of them all their strength to keep him where they wanted him.

'For God's sake, shut him up!'

'Pack it in, you idiot!'

'Cripes, where's that scarf?'

The hands descended on his face, suffocating him, stifling his screams with mouthfuls of woollen windings and mufflings until he could feel all the panic literally stuffed down his throat, exploding in his breast. He was out of control and knew it, fighting with his own terror which he knew was more dangerous in the confined space than anything more his assailants could do to him. They pressed him down, angrily, their cool as much disturbed as his own, swearing and arguing and clumsy, and closed the lid hard down on his back. The whole box was thickly lined with foam rubber, and Jonathan, rolled up like a woodlouse, felt himself insulated, entombed, utterly divorced from the world and all reality. He was on his own, and by his own efforts he knew he would survive, or not – an entirely salutary realisation, for his desperation was using up an unnecessary amount of the meagre air supply. His own breathing was the only noise he could hear, wheezing with great difficulty through his stifled air passages; his nose, upside-down, was having a job to cope, and needed every bit of help it could get, by his being very calm and relaxed. He knew all this, even while he could feel trickles of the hot sweat of fear running down his body. It was like being two people, the strong, implacable one, knowing what he must do, trying to crush the instinctive self, wild with fright. It was a battle on its own going on in the box, quite apart from anything that might be happening outside which at that moment truly didn't concern him. He could feel the box being moved, carried, put down, moved again, kicked. He thought he could hear people talking, the transistor radio playing, someone laughing, an engine starting up, but none of it mattered to his private struggle. The foam rubber seemed to be bulging into all the few spaces his body had left and sucking the air into its thick, hot substance, denying him his right to it. He thought only of breathing; there was nothing else to distract him. It was very hard, and he didn't see how he was going to even notice if he lost consciousness, because there was so little to show for being alive, except the spreading pain of cramps which he would be only too happy to forego. There was, curiously, no sense of time at all: time was only as long as he could breathe, and time was running out. He started to feel terribly hot, burning all over, and he couldn't hear himself breathing any more, but only his pulses thumping. He tried to ration his breathing, making it very shallow, but he couldn't hear it or feel it for the throbbing in his head, and he realised that there was nothing he could do now to help himself: it was beyond his control. The thumping and the throbbing was all there was, bursting in his ears and his throat and his eyeballs. The box no longer seemed to contain him: he was unconscious of confinement, of pain, of even *being*. Only the pounding was real, swelling monstrously, burning, killing.

Afterwards he remembered he had always thought of suffocation as an innocuous death, as deaths went. Not very intelligent really. He never thought that again. The air was cool and beautiful, smelling of the sea. He realised after a bit that the gasping, whimpering noise was himself – coming to, perhaps. He couldn't see, but he could breathe, move, even his hands. How long had he been? He was lying down, and there was a strange, unfamiliar motion beneath him, and strange noises going on. He struggled feebly on to his side.

'Thank God for that,' somebody said, close to. 'I'll leave him to you now, Jamie. Try him with a drop of brandy. He'll be OK.'

'Oh, Jesus!' said Jamie softly, not blaspheming, but in thankfulness. 'I didn't reckon on that. We nearly suffocated him. Can you hear me, lad?'

from *Prove Yourself a Hero* by K. M. Peyton

* What impression do you get of Jonathan before he panics? What sort of person is he?

* What signs are there that once he is in the box Jonathan is giving up the struggle to remain calm and survive?

* What signs are there that the kidnappers are nervous?

* How do you know that the kidnappers have prepared for their task very carefully?

* There are at least two things for which they are **not** prepared. What are they?

* One paragraph in this extract is very long. Why hasn't the writer divided it up? Would it change the effect it has on you if she **had** divided it up?

* Later on in the story Jonathan feels very ashamed of the way he panicked during this incident. Was he right to feel ashamed?

* The book from which this extract is taken is called *Prove Yourself a Hero*. Can you suggest any reasons for the title from reading this extract?

1. Imagine Jamie is caught. He has to make a statement about what happened. Look carefully at the extract to decide what part Jamie played in the kidnapping and then write the part of his statement which deals with just this incident.

2. It often happens that when people recall moments of panic or crisis they say that things seemed to happen very slowly at the time. Look at the paragraph beginning 'The hands descended on his face . . .' At this point Jonathan is in a state of panic. The writer shows this by describing his thoughts and feelings during these moments in great detail, as if time had actually slowed down.

Write a similar description of someone's thoughts or feelings during a time of crisis or danger. You may decide to base the writing on your own experience.

3. Write a story about someone whose greatest fear is of being shut into a confined space but who has to go through such a claustrophobic experience, for example:

> in a lift stuck between floors
> during a pot-holing expedition
> in a submarine
> during a breakdown in an underground train
> hiding from someone in a cupboard or box.

Phobias

One can have a phobia about almost anything from snakes to string. But basically phobias fall into three broad categories. First, fear of a specific object, such as a cat or spider. Second, a fear of a specific situation, such as being in a place like a restaurant; or going to school; or going anywhere outside the home. Third, and more abstract, a fear of a specific illness, or death.

Much still remains to be answered about the causes of phobias. Why, for instance, should one child develop a phobia of spiders after one is put down his or her neck, while another, after a similar incident, remains unaffected? And what about those people who can give no reason whatsoever to explain their phobia? Why should natural childhood fears, like fears of strangers or the dark, remain into adulthood with some, and not with others? And why might a build-up of stress cause agoraphobia in some instances, but not in others?

Although the causes of a phobia may differ, the effect on all phobics, faced with what they fear, is the same – varying only in degree. They get a panic attack, with its attendant sensations: breathlessness, pounding heart, dizziness or fainting, tenseness, sweating, a feeling of remoteness. Their reaction is, naturally enough, to avoid getting into the same situation again, and this can seriously curtail their activities. They may also interpret these frightening sensations as symptoms of an illness, and go to the doctor for treatment, under the impression they are going mad, or having a heart attack.

adapted from *Phobias and Obsessions* by Joy Melville

* Joy Melville makes three broad categories of phobias. Below is a list of phobias which people sometimes suffer from. Which categories do they fall into?

acrophobia — fear of heights
agoraphobia — fear of open spaces
arachnophobia — fear of spiders
claustrophobia — fear of enclosed space
xenophobia — fear of strangers
cardiophobia — fear of heart disease
demonophobia — fear of devils or demons
aerophobia — fear of flying
hippophobia — fear of horses
bacilliphobia — fear of microbes
hypnophobia — fear of sleep

hydrophobia   — fear of water
ornithophobia — fear of birds
entomophobia — fear of insects
necrophobia   — fear of death
zoophobia   — fear of animals
autophobia   — fear of oneself

* Why (according to Joy Melville) do people misinterpret the symptoms of phobia and go to the doctor thinking that they are suffering from **other** illnesses?

* Can you recall being very much afraid of something when you were a little child which worries you only a little (or not at all) now? How did you conquer the fear?

1. Look at what happens to Jonathan when he is shut into the box in the extract from *Prove Yourself a Hero* on page 7. What happens to him which shows that he is suffering the kind of panic attack described here, as well as being uncomfortable and short of air? Quote words and phrases from both *Prove Yourself a Hero* and *Phobias and Obsessions* to show the connections.

A New Fear

Beyond our boundaries on that side the country was new to me. I followed unfamiliar paths past kopjes[1] that till now had been part of the jagged horizon, hazed with distance. It was a wide green valley, where a small river sparkled, and vivid water-birds darted over the rushes. The grass was thick and soft to my calves, the trees stood tall and shapely.

It was very silent: a hot morning with pigeons cooing throatily, the midday shadows lying dense and thick with clear yellow spaces of sunlight between and in all that wide green park-like valley, not a human soul but myself.

I was listening to the quick regular tapping of a woodpecker when slowly a chill feeling seemed to grow up from the small of my back to my shoulders, in a constricting spasm like a shudder, and at the roots of my hair a tingling sensation began and ran down over the surface of my flesh, leaving me goosefleshed and cold, though I was damp with sweat. Fever? I thought; then uneasily, turned to look over my shoulder; and realised suddenly that this was fear. It was extraordinary, even humiliating. It was a new fear.

I had read of this feeling, how the bigness and silence of Africa, under the ancient sun, grows dense and takes shape in the mind, till even the birds seem to call menacingly, and a deadly spirit comes out of the trees and the rocks. You move warily, as if your very passing disturbs something old and evil, something dark and big and angry that might suddenly rear and strike from behind. You look at groves of entwined trees, and picture the animals that might be lurking there; you look at the river running slowly, dropping from level to level through the vlei,[2] spreading into pools where at night the buck come to drink, and the crocodiles rise and drag them by their soft noses into underwater caves. Fear possessed me. I found I was turning round and round, because of that shapeless menace behind me that might reach out and take me; I kept glancing at the files of kopjes which, seen from a different angle, seemed to change with every step. I did not know where I was. I was lost. Panic seized me. I found I was spinning round and round, staring anxiously at this tree and that, peering up at the sun which appeared to have moved into an eastern slant, shedding the sad yellow light of sunset. Hours must have passed! I looked at my watch and found that this state of meaningless terror had lasted perhaps ten minutes.

from *The Old Chief Mshlanga* by Doris Lessing

[1] *low hills*
[2] *low-lying ground*

* Is the storyteller actually being threatened by anything? Is she in danger? Is she just being silly or can you sympathise with her feelings?

1. Have you ever felt fear or panic without a particular cause? Write about your experience, or write a story about someone who has such an experience.

* Fear of the unknown . . .
  fear of being lost . . .
  fear of not being recognised . . .
  fear of being alone . . .
  fear of open spaces . . .
  fear of being watched . . .

  Which of these best describes the storyteller's feelings? There may be more than one. Can you add to the list?

* What does the storyteller find frightening about the countryside? She describes this as a **new** fear. Why might she never have felt it before?

* The storyteller calls this **'meaningless'** terror. Why?

* What does the storyteller mean by **'fear possessed me'**?

* Several times the storyteller turns round and round. Why?

* Could this feeling happen to someone in the middle of a big city? Can any place suddenly seem terrifying?

2. Have you ever felt panic in any of these situations:
    in an examination
    having forgotten something
    knowing you're going to be late
    being given an anaesthetic
    losing your balance
    being in the same room as a creature that you are frightened of
    being totally alone
    being singled out from a crowd by name
    waking up from a nightmare
    waiting for someone who is very late?

Write about your experience.

The Tower

'The road begins to rise in a series of gentle curves, passing through pleasing groves of olives and vines. 5 km. on the left is the fork to Florence. To the right may be seen the Tower of Sacrifice (470 steps) built in 1535 by Niccolo di Ferramano; superstitious fear left the tower intact when, in 1549, the surrounding village was completely destroyed . . .'

. . . 'I've just got time to look at the tower,' Caroline said aloud, as she put the guide-book back in the pigeon-hole under the dashboard, and drove carefully along the gentle road until she came to the fork for Florence on the left.

On the top of a little hill to the right stood a tall round tower. There was no other building in sight. In a land where every available piece of ground is cultivated, there was no cultivated ground around this tower. On the left was the fork to Florence: on the right a track led up to the top of the hill.

Caroline knew that she wanted to take the fork to the left, to Florence and home and Neville and – said an urgent voice inside her – for safety. This voice so much shocked her that she got out of the car and began to trudge up the dusty track towards the tower.

After all, I may not come this way again, she argued; it seems silly to miss the chance of seeing it when I've already got a reason for being interested. I'm only just going to have a quick look – and she glanced at the setting sun, telling herself that she would indeed have to be quick if she were to get back to Florence before dark.

And now she had climbed the hill and was standing in front of the tower. It was built of narrow red bricks, and only thin slits pierced its surface right up to the top where Caroline could see some kind of narrow platform encircling it. Before her was an arched doorway. I'm just going to have a quick look, she assured herself again, and then she walked in.

She was in an empty room with a low arched ceiling. A narrow stone staircase clung to the wall and circled round the room to disappear through a hole in the ceiling.

'There ought to be a wonderful view at the top,' said Caroline firmly to herself, and she laid her hand on the rusty rail and started to climb, and as she climbed, she counted.

'– thirty-nine, forty, forty-one,' she said and with the forty-first step she came through the ceiling and saw over her head, far, far above, the deep blue evening sky, a small circle of blue framed in a narrowing shaft round which the narrow staircase spiralled. There was no inner wall; only the rusty rail protected the climber on the inside.

'– eighty-three, eighty-four –' counted Caroline. The sky above her was losing its colour and she wondered why the narrow slit windows in the wall had all been placed so that they spiralled round the staircase too high for anyone climbing it to see through them.

'It's getting dark very quickly,' said Caroline at the hundred-and-fiftieth step. 'I know what the tower is like now. It would be much more sensible to give up and go home.'

At the two-hundred-and-sixty-ninth step, her hand, moving forward on the rail, met only empty space. For an interminable second she shivered, pressing back to the hard brick on the other side. Then hesitantly she groped forwards, upwards, and at last her fingers met the rusty rail again, and again she climbed.

But now the breaks in the rail became more and more frequent. Sometimes she had to climb several steps with her left shoulder pressed tightly against the brick wall before her searching hand could find the tenuous rusty comfort again.

At the three-hundred-and-seventy-fifth step, the rail, as her moving hand clutched it, crumpled away under her fingers. 'I'd better just go by the wall,' she told herself, and now her left hand traced the rough brick as she climbed up and up.

'Four-hundred-and-twenty-two, four-hundred-and-twenty-three,' counted Caroline with part of her brain. 'I really ought to go down now,' said another part, 'I wish – oh, I want to go down now –' but she could not. 'It would be so silly to give up,' she told herself, desperately trying to rationalise what drove her on. 'Just because one's afraid –' and then she had to stifle that thought too and there was nothing left in her brain but the steadily mounting tally of the steps.

'–four-hundred-and-seventy!' said Caroline aloud with relief, and then she stopped abruptly because the steps had stopped too. There was nothing ahead but a piece of broken railing barring her way, and the sky drained now of all its colour, was still some twenty feet above her head.

'But how idiotic,' she said to the air. 'The whole thing's absolutely pointless,' and then the fingers of her left hand, exploring the wall beside her, met not brick but wood.

She turned to see what it was, and then in the wall, level with the top step, was a small wooden door. 'So it does go somewhere after all,' she said, and she fumbled with the rusty handle. The door pushed open and she stepped through.

She was on a narrow stone platform about a yard wide. It seemed to encircle the tower. The platform sloped downwards away from the tower and its stones were very smooth and shiny – and this was all she noticed before she looked beyond the stones and down.

She was immeasurably, unbelievably high and alone and the ground below was a world away. It was not credible, not possible that she should be so far from the ground. All her being was suddenly absorbed in the single impulse to hurl herself from the sloping platform. 'I cannot go down any other way,' she said, and then she heard what she said and stepped back, clutching the soft rotten wood of the doorway with hands sodden

with sweat. There is no other way, said the voice in her brain, there is no other way.

'This is vertigo,' said Caroline. 'I've only got to close my eyes and keep still for a minute and it will pass off. It's bound to pass off. I've never had it before but I know what it is and it's vertigo.' She closed her eyes and kept very still and felt the cold sweat running down her body.

'I should be all right now,' she said at last, and carefully she stepped back through the doorway onto the four-hundred-and-seventieth step and pulled the door shut behind her. She looked up at the sky, swiftly darkening with night. Then, for the first time, she looked down into the shaft of the tower, down to the narrow unprotected staircase spiralling round and round and round, and disappearing into the dark. She said – she screamed – 'I can't go down.'

She stood still on the top step, staring downwards, and slowly the last light faded from the tower. She could not move. It was not possible that she should dare to go down, step by step down the unprotected stairs into the dark below. It would be much easier to fall, said the voice in her head, to take one step to the left and fall and it would be all over. You cannot climb down.

She began to cry, shuddering with the pain of her sobs. It could not be true that she had brought herself to this peril, that there could be no safety for her unless she could climb down the menacing stairs. The reality *must* be that she was safe at home with Neville – but this was the reality and here were the stairs; at last she stopped crying and said, 'Now I shall go down.'

'One!' she counted and, her right hand tearing at the brick wall, she moved first one and then the other foot down to the second step. 'Two!' she counted, and then she thought of the depth below her and stood still, stupified with terror. The stone beneath her feet, the brick against her hand were too frail protections for her exposed body. They could not save her from the voice that repeated that it would be easier to fall. Abruptly she sat down on the step.

'Two,' she counted again, and spreading both her hands tightly against the step on each side of her, she swung her body off the second step, down on the third, 'Three,' she counted, then 'four' then 'five', pressing closer and closer into the wall, away from the empty drop on the other side.

At the twenty-first step she said, 'I think I can do it now.' She slid her right hand up the rough wall and slowly stood upright. Then with her other hand she reached for the railing it was now too dark to see, but it was not there.

For timeless time she stood there, knowing nothing but fear. 'Twenty-one,' she said, 'twenty-one,' over and over again, but she could not step onto the twenty-second stair.

Something brushed her face. She knew it was a bat, not a hand, that touched but still it was horror beyond conceivable horror, and it was this horror, without any sense of moving from dread to safety, that at last impelled her down the stairs.

'Twenty-three, twenty-four, twenty-five –' she counted, and around her the air was full of whispering skin-stretched wings. If one of them should touch her again, she must fall. 'Twenty-six, twenty-seven, twenty-eight –' The skin of her right hand was torn and hot with blood, for she would never lift it from the wall, only press it slowly down and force her rigid legs to move from the knowledge of each step to the peril of the next.

140 So Caroline came down the dark tower. She could not think. She could know nothing but fear. Only her brain remorselessly recorded the tally. 'Five-hundred-and-one,' it counted, 'five-hundred-and-two – and three – and four –'

from *The Tower* by Marghanita Laski

* What has happened to Caroline at the end of the story?

* Why do you think the tower was called the 'Tower of Sacrifice'?

* Would **you** have climbed the tower . . . .?

* What signs are there in the story that the tower is evil and menacing?

1. Write a story about someone who accepts or is drawn into a challenge which ends in panic.

A Closer Look

1. How does the phrase 'superstitious fear' in the extract from the guide-book (lines 1 to 5) prepare you for what is to come?

2. Is it important that 'gentle curves' (line 1) and 'pleasing groves' (line 2) are mentioned before the 'Tower of Sacrifice'?

3. What hint of something sinister about the tower are we given in paragraph two? (lines 10 to 14)

4. Between lines 15 and 33 there are four occasions when Caroline ignores possible warnings and persuades herself to continue into the tower. What are these occasions? Why does the writer include them?

5. Why does the writer repeatedly remind us of the number of steps which Caroline climbs?

6. Count the number of times the writer reminds us of the gathering darkness. Why does she do this?

7. The reader is often reminded that Caroline is a sensible, intelligent person. How does this reinforce the horror of what happens to her?

8. Caroline seems at times to be literally in two minds about what she is doing. Why are her thoughts split in this way?

Where is the man running to?
What is he escaping from?
What have his eyes seen?
What has caused the house to split?
What is in the lake?

Give the picture a title.
Write about the picture in any way you like.

Is the figure fleeing from something?
Why are the hands pressed to the ears?
Why are the eyes so pale and staring?
Why is the mouth open so wide?
Who are the two people behind?
What will happen next?

Give the picture a title.
Write about the picture in any way you like.

Poem

In the stump of the old tree, where the heart has rotted out, there is a hole the length of a man's arm, and a dank pool at the bottom of it where the rain gathers, and the old leaves turn into lacy skeletons. But do not put your hand down to see, because

in the stumps of old trees, where the hearts have rotted out, there are holes the length of a man's arm, and dank pools at the bottom where the rain gathers and old leaves turn to lace, and the beak of a dead bird gapes like a trap. But do not put your hand down to see, because

in the stumps of old trees with rotten hearts, where the rain gathers and the laced leaves and the dead bird like a trap, there are holes the length of a man's arm, and in every crevice of the rotten wood grow weasel's eyes like molluscs, their lids open and shut with the tide. But do not put your hand down to see, because

in the stumps of old trees where the rain gathers and the trapped leaves and the beak, and the laced weasel's eyes, there are holes the length of a man's arm, and at the bottom a sodden bible written in the language of rooks. But do not put your hand down to see, because

in the stumps of old trees where the hearts have rotted out there are holes the length of a man's arm where the weasels are trapped and the letters of the rook language are laced on the sodden leaves, and at the bottom there is a man's arm. But do not put your hand down to see, because

in the stumps of old trees where the hearts have rotted out there are deep holes and dank pools where the rain gathers, and if you ever put your hand down to see, you can wipe it in the sharp grass till it bleeds, but you'll never want to eat with it again.

Hugh Sykes Davies

Making it Clear

1. Sometimes a writer wants to describe very clearly how something is done so the reader can understand it easily. Below are two descriptions of this kind taken from stories. Read each one and draw what the writer is describing. Compare your drawings with those of someone else in the class. If the drawings are not very similar discuss whether this is because you have not completely understood the description, or because you have not drawn it accurately or because the writer has not described it carefully enough.

Our trolleys were simple vehicles for getting a good ride downhill at a fast speed. To make one you had to get a stout piece of wood about five feet in length and eighteen inches wide. Then you needed four wheels, preferably two pairs, large ones for the back and smaller ones for the front. However, since we bought our wheels from the scrapyard, most trolleys had four odd wheels. Now you had to get a hole through the wood at the front. Usually it would take three or four attempts to get the hole bored through. Through this hole you fitted the giant nut-and-bolt, which acted as a swivel for the steering. Fastened to the nut was a strip of wood, on to which the front axle was secured by bent nails. A piece of rope tied to each end of the axle served for steering. Then a knob of margarine had to be slanced out of the kitchen to grease the wheels and bearings. Next you had to paint a name on it: 'Invincible' or 'Dreadnought', though it might be a motto: 'Death before Dishonour' or 'Labour and Wait'. That done, you then stuck your chest out, opened the back gate, and wheeled your trolley out to face the critical eyes of the world.

from *The Goal Keeper's Revenge* by Bill Naughton

To make a simple bird-trap, cut a bendy stick and tie a string to one end. Then sharpen the other, so that it can impale a fruit as bait. Just at the base of this point flatten it a little, and bore a hole through the flat part. Cut a little peg that will just stick in the mouth of this hole. Then make a loop in the end of the string: bend the stick, as in stringing a bow, till the loop will thread through the little hole, and jam it with the peg, along which the loop should lie spread. Bait the point, and hang it in a tree among the twigs: the bird alights on the peg to peck the fruit, the pegs falls out, the loop whips tight round its ankles.

from *A High Wind in Jamaica* by Richard Hughes

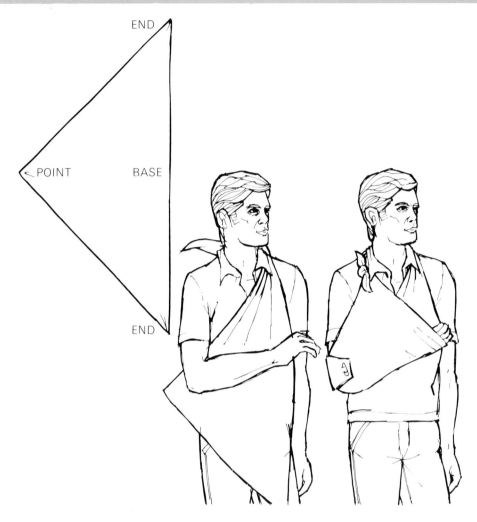

2. Look carefully at the diagrams above and then write the instructions you would give to someone who wanted to make a sling for an injured right arm but who could not see these diagrams.

3. When you make coffee directly from ground coffee beans rather than from instant coffee powder or granules, you have to let the hot water soak up the flavour of the coffee for several minutes. Usually the coffee is made in a jug or pot and then filtered so that the bitter-tasting coffee grounds which have not dissolved are not poured into the cup with the coffee. In France, some people make coffee without a jug or pot using the method shown on the next page.

Look carefully at the illustrations and then describe stage by stage how you would make a cup of coffee by this method.

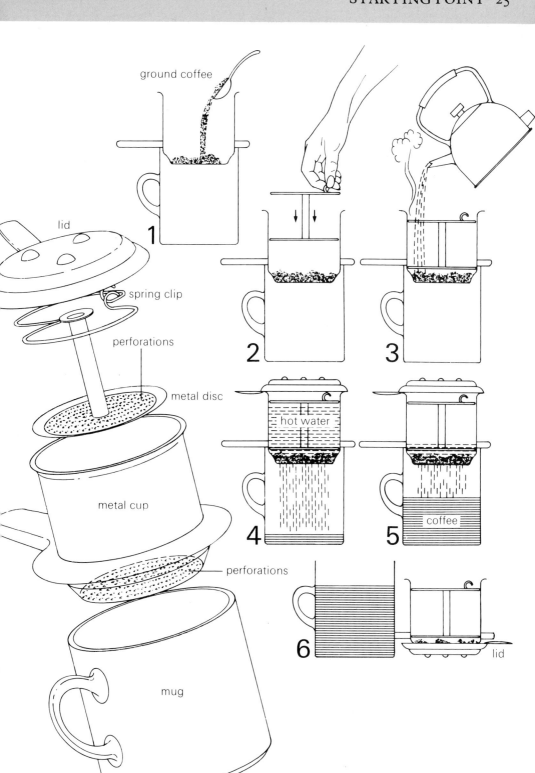

ground coffee

1

lid

spring clip

perforations

metal disc

metal cup

perforations

mug

2

3

4

hot water

5

coffee

6

lid

THE HAPPIEST DAYS OF
YOUR LIFE?

Why Do You Go to School?

* Do you go to school in order to:

>   be trained for a job
>   pass examinations
>   learn skills and subjects which may help you to make good use of
>   your leisure time
>   develop your physical and mental abilities
>   introduce you to new ideas and theories
>   help you to organise your own lives
>   learn how to live and work with other people
>   learn how to think for yourselves?

* In most schools pupils spend between two and three hours on compulsory Maths and English each week, and one or two hours each week studying some of the following subjects:

>   foreign languages
>   sciences
>   physical education
>   religious education
>   history
>   geography
>   crafts
>   art
>   music
>   homecrafts.

What other subjects which are not usually studied do you think ought to be available? Look at your list of possible reasons for attending school to help you make suggestions.

   Discuss this with a partner and defend your ideas.

* What subjects which you study at the moment would you give up if you could, and why?

1. Draw up an 'ideal' timetable and write a few paragraphs to support your suggestions. Remember that only about five hours are available for lessons each day.

The Fun They Had

Margie even wrote about it that night in her diary. On the page headed May 17, 2157, she wrote, 'Today Tommy found a real book!'

It was a very old book. Margie's grandfather once said that when he was a little boy *his* grandfather told him that there was a time when all stories were printed on paper.

They turned the pages, which were yellow and crinkly, and it was awfully funny to read words that stood still instead of moving the way they were supposed to on a screen, you know. And then, when they turned back to the page before, it had the same words on it that it had had when they read it the first time.

'Gee,' said Tommy, 'what a waste. When you're through with the book, you just throw it away, I guess. Our television screen must have had a million books on it and it's good for plenty more. I wouldn't throw *it* away.'

'Same with mine,' said Margie. She was eleven and hadn't seen as many textbooks as Tommy had. He was thirteen.

She said, 'Where did you find it?'

'In my house.' He pointed without looking, because he was busy reading. 'In the attic.'

'What's it about?'

'School.'

Margie was scornful. 'School? What's there to write about school? I hate school.'

Margie always hated school, but now she hated it more than ever. The mechanical teacher had been giving her test after test in geography and she had been doing worse and worse until her mother had shaken her head sorrowfully and sent for the County Inspector.

He was a round little man with a red face and a whole box of tools with dials and wires. He smiled at Margie and gave her an apple, then took the teacher apart. Margie had hoped he wouldn't know how to put it together again, but he knew how all right, and, after an hour or so, there it was again, large and black and ugly, with a big screen on which all the lessons were shown and the questions were asked. That wasn't so bad. The part Margie hated most was the slot where she had to put homework and test papers. She always had to write them out in a punch code they made her learn when she was six years old, and the mechanical teacher calculated the mark in no time.

The Inspector had smiled after he was finished and patted Margie's head. He said to her mother, 'It's not the little girl's fault, Mrs Jones. I think the geography sector was geared a little too quick. Those things happen sometimes. I've slowed it up to an average ten-year level. Actually, the over-all pattern of her progress is quite satisfactory.' And he patted Margie's head again.

Margie was disappointed. She had been hoping they would take the teacher away altogether. They had once taken Tommy's teacher away for nearly a month because the history sector had blanked out completely.

So she said to Tommy, 'Why would anyone write about school?'

Tommy looked at her with very superior eyes. 'Because it's not our kind of school, stupid. This is the old kind of school that they had hundreds and hundreds of years ago.' He added loftily, pronouncing the word carefully, '*Centuries* ago.'

Margie was hurt. 'Well, I don't know what kind of school they had all that time ago.' She read the book over his shoulder for a while, then said, 'Anyway, they had a teacher.'

'Sure they had a teacher, but it wasn't a *regular* teacher. It was a man.'

'A man? How could a man be a teacher?'

'Well, he just told the boys and girls things and gave them homework and asked them questions.'

'A man isn't smart enough.'

'Sure he is. My father knows as much as my teacher.'

'He can't. A man can't know as much as a teacher.'

'He knows almost as much, I betcha.'

Margie wasn't prepared to dispute that. She said, 'I wouldn't want a strange man in my house to teach me.'

Tommy screamed with laughter. 'You don't know much, Margie. The teachers didn't live in the house. They had a special building and all the kids went there.'

'And all the kids learned the same thing?'

'Sure, if they were the same age.'

'But my mother says a teacher has to be adjusted to fit the mind of each boy and girl it teaches and that each kid has to be taught differently.'

'Just the same they didn't do it that way then. If you don't like it, you don't have to read the book.'

'I didn't say I didn't like it,' Margie said quickly. She wanted to read about those funny schools.

They weren't even half-finished when Margie's mother called, 'Margie! School!'

Margie looked up. 'Not yet, Mamma.'

'Now!' said Mrs Jones. 'And it's probably time for Tommy too.'

Margie said to Tommy, 'Can I read the book some more with you after school?'

'Maybe,' he said nonchalantly. He walked away whistling, the dusty old book tucked beneath his arm.

Margie went into the schoolroom. It was right next to her bedroom, and the mechanical teacher was on and waiting for her. It was always on at the same time every day except Saturday and Sunday, because her mother said little girls learned better if they learned at regular hours.

The screen was lit up, and it said: 'Today's arithmetic lesson is on the addition of proper fractions. Please insert yesterday's homework in the proper slot.'

Margie did so with a sigh. She was thinking about the old schools they had when her grandfather's gradfather was a little boy. All the kids from the whole neighbourhood came, laughing and shouting in the schoolyard, sitting together in the schoolroom, going home together at the end of the day. They learned the same things, so they could help one another on the homework and talk about it.

And the teachers were people . . . The mechanical teacher was flashing on the screen: 'When we add the fractions $\frac{1}{2}$ and $\frac{1}{4}$ –'

Margie was thinking about how the kids must have loved it in the old days. She was thinking about the fun they had.

from *Earth is Room Enough* by Isaac Asimov

* In the story, Margie has got only part of the picture of what schools were like in the twentieth century. If you wanted to give her a clearer and fuller picture, what would you tell her?

* What does Margie dislike about her schooling? Is she better or worse off than you are? If teaching and learning went on through video screens at home, what would you be pleased to miss through not being at school, and what would you be sorry to miss?

* What was the best lesson you ever had? What made it so good?

* What advantages do books have over video screens, and what advantages do video screens have over books?

* If teaching machines of a very advanced kind — like those in the story — were available for schools today, what subjects would you use them for? What subjects and topics do you think would not be suitable for machines to teach? Why?

* Take a good, long look at the exercise books that are in your bag or desk. If they were all that was left of your school in two hundred years' time, what would people living then learn about life in school today?

1. What might schools be like in about two hundred years from now? Write about one pupil's typical day in a school in the year 2199.

2. Sometimes, when a new building is being constructed a 'time capsule' (a sealed box) is buried in the foundations. The box contains objects which represent life at the time of their burial.

What objects would you want to put into such a time capsule to represent your school this year?

The School Report

THE VALLEY COMPREHENSIVE SCHOOL

Report for the half year ending 28 February 1983

Name SHARON HOLMES   Form 5TK   Age 15·6   Average Age 16·2

Absences 8   Times Late 14

Subject	Effort	Grade	Comment	
English	C	D+	Sharon has some ability, but must work much harder if she is to pass 'O' level.	MK
Mathematics	D	D	Sharon makes little effort and her work shows only a poor understanding.	JS.
French	D	E	a consistently weak performance.	CD.
German				
History				
Geography	C+	C	Sharon has done some quite good work.	FC
Biology	C	C	Fair progress	HC
Physics or Chemistry	δ	δ	Sharon does not show any interest.	P.R.
Religious Education	C	C	Rather disappointing	J.L.
Woodwork or Domestic Science	C+	C+	Good. Sharon has continued to work modestly but well.	ANC
Metalwork or Needlecraft	D	D	Untidy and disorganised	PE
Art	D	G	Little has been attempted, less achieved!	AW
Physical Education	C	C	Fair	CH

Really this is a disappointing report. I had hoped that Sharon would appreciate the importance of this year's work and make a greater effort, but this has not been the case. Too often her mind seems Form Teacher M Keble
preoccupied with other things.

Sharon is allowing important educational opportunities to pass her by. She *must* make a determined effort before it is too late—— Headmaster KJ Lenden

* What do you think of Sharon Holmes's report?

* What does the report tell you about her?

* If this were **your** report, what would your parents say to you about it?

* Assuming that the Effort and Grade marks on Sharon's report are accurate, what does it tell you about her school and her teachers?

Sharon has brought home her school report. She has opened the sealed envelope it was in and her mother is angry because of this and because the report is a disappointing one.

Sharon stayed in her room, the door closed but not locked. She made no attempt to go down for tea, neither did her mother call her. She switched on her small transistor radio and listened to Capital for a few minutes. She switched it off again and began to doodle on the front of a school exercise book.

At half past five she heard her father come in. Bracing herself for his voice summoning her on his arrival outside her room, all that she heard were voices talking urgently and then, after five minutes or so, the television going on.

Her father always liked to watch the news.

At six o'clock, the sound went off again.

Sharon broke the point of her pencil against the book cover. She half thought she would go downstairs and have it out with them. Keeping her waiting like that.

'Sharon!'

She opened the door slowly and stepped outside. At the bottom of the brown stair carpet, her father stood tapping his left hand impatiently against his leg.

'Come down here.'

She tried not to look at his grey eyes, unusually stern. He'd changed out of his work clothes into a pair of shapeless brown trousers and the same chunky green cardigan he always wore around the house.

'Come in here.'

He stood by the living-room door and ushered Sharon past him. Her mother was sitting in her armchair on the far side of the fire. She was wearing her glasses, the ones she used for reading. Her face looked strained, tense.

'Sit down.'

Sharon went over and sat on the settee, tucking one leg behind the other and pulling her skirt down at the hem. Her father looked at her for a few moments, without speaking. Then he sat in the chair on the other side of the fire.

The front of the fire was switched on, so that the orange light glowed and the metal fan behind it turned, giving a flickering effect. Neither of the bars was on.

The living-room door was ajar.

On the low coffee-table, in the middle of the room, lay the report. The two ends, where it had been folded, pushed upwards: it looked like a stranded bird.

'Well?'

Sharon blinked at her father and shook her head once, not meaning anything.

'Tell your father what you've done.'

Mr Holmes looked across the table at his wife quickly, as though annoyed that she'd interrupted. 'Well, Sharon, I'm waiting,' he said.

Sharon sniffed. 'What for?'

'Don't answer your father back!'

'Maureen, don't . . .'

'What d'you want me to say? You know what I did. You can see. What's the point of me saying it?'

Sharon was leaning forward, staring at her father. 'Jack, don't let her . . .'

'That's right, you let her tell you what to do. Just like . . .'

He jumped from his chair and slapped her round the face. Sharon fell backwards, then sideways, both hands to her cheek, the tears smarting in her eyes.

'Jack! You shouldn't have!'

'Shut up, Maureen! For God's sake, shut up!'

Still crying, Sharon heard her mother hurry out of the room, shutting the door with a bang. She knew her father was standing over her and she kept her face hidden inside her hands, sobbing and shaking. Her cheek was stinging and she was breathing unevenly.

'Sharon.'

She could sense him leaning over her and when he put his hand on her shoulder she flinched. He pulled the hand away quickly and moved back to the fire.

'I lost my temper. I'm sorry.'

Sharon sat up a little more, still not looking round. She rubbed at her eyes, reaching under the sleeve of her jumper for a crumpled tissue.

'Come on, Sharon, it wasn't that hard.'

She turned and looked up at him. No, it hadn't been that hard. It had been the shock, the surprise. He hadn't hit her since she was a little girl and she's lied about stealing sweets from a jar in the kitchen. She'd been seven and afterwards he'd picked her up and held her in his arms and cuddled her.

While they were like that, her mother came back into the room. She was smoking, a thing she rarely did, and her mouth was drawn in tightly. She stepped between them and sat back in her chair without looking at either of them.

Somewhere outside a dog barked.

'Why did you do it, Sharon?'

'I didn't think it mattered. All of the other kids open theirs.'

'That's not an answer, is it?'

'She did it because she was ashamed of what was in it.' Her mother's voice was bitter, edgy.

'If I was ashamed of it, what would I want to look at it for?'

'Don't you raise your voice to me, young lady, or I'll get your father to give you another backhander!'

'Yes, you would!'

They were both standing, leaning slightly forwards, eyes bright. Mr Holmes stepped past the table and took hold of his wife by the shoulders.

'Maureen, that won't do any good.'

'Won't it? Perhaps if you'd done it more often she wouldn't be in the mess she is now.'

'I'm not in a mess,' Sharon shouted defiantly.

Her father ignored her, shaking his head, his hands still on his wife's shoulders.

'Maureen.'

'What?' she snapped.

'All that won't help now.'

She shot him a fierce glance: 'No, it won't, will it?'

She shook herself free and sat down heavily, knocking her glasses from the arm of the chair on to the carpet. He bent down and picked them up, replacing them.

'I'll make some tea,' he said.

All the while he was in the kitchen, Sharon and her mother didn't look at one another. Mrs Holmes smoked another cigarette and Sharon watched the movements of the electric fire.

When they'd all started their first cup, Mr Holmes reached down and picked up the report. He looked at it and set it down on his lap.

'All right, Sharon, we'll forget the fact that you opened it when you shouldn't have.'

'No, we . . .'

'We'll forget all about that. But what about the report itself?'

Sharon put her cup down in the saucer, rattling it against the spoon. She didn't know what to say.

'I mean,' her father went on, 'it isn't very good, is it?'

'Not very good!' said her mother quickly. 'It's awful!'

He looked across at her. 'Now, Maureen, it's not that bad.'

'Well, I don't see how it could be much worse.'

Sharon sighed and they both looked at her.

'Why haven't you been working?' her father asked.

'I have.'

'Not according to this, you haven't.'

'Oh, teachers are never satisfied.'

'But you've got such low grades. There isn't anything over a C.'

'C's average.'

'Well, you're better than average.'

'They don't think so.'

'When you were at junior school,' Mrs Holmes said, 'you were always coming top in things. You used to get ever such good reports. You got a prize once.'

'It wasn't a prize, Mum, it was a book for helping in the library.'

'That's beside the point, Sharon,' said her father. 'What I want to know is why everyone says you could have done better.'

'Because they always say that.'

'Not if they don't mean it.'

'And what about your exams?' asked her mother sharply. 'It doesn't sound as if you're going to pass anything.'

Sharon opened her mouth to say something but thought better of it. Her mother got up and took the report from her husband's lap. She sat down with it and put on her glasses.

Mr Holmes glanced quickly at Sharon, then poured out some more tea.

'You see what the headmaster says . . .' her mother began.

'What does he know about it?'

Mrs Holmes slapped the report against her knee. 'That only goes to show what an ignorant little madam you are.'

'He doesn't even know who I am.'

'Of course he does. What do you think he's paid for?'

'Oh, Mum!'

Mrs Holmes glanced at the report again. 'What about Mrs Keble, then?'

'Miss.'

'Miss Keble, whatever she is. She knows you well enough, I suppose?'

Sharon shrugged her shoulders.

'See what she says – "disappointing".' She tapped the paper with her other hand. ' "Preoccupied with other things." What have you got to say about that?'

'Nothing.'

'What sort of other things, Sharon?' asked her father.

'I don't know, Dad.' Voice rising again. 'I didn't write it, did I? You'd better ask her.'

As soon as the words were out of her mouth, Sharon wanted to swallow them back. But her father carried on as though she hadn't said it.

'Well, what have you been thinking about when you should have been paying attention to your work?'

'I told you, I don't . . .'

'It's that boy, that's who it is,' interrupted her mother with a note almost of triumph.

'What boy?'

'Which boy is this, Sharon?'

'The boy she's been going out with.'

'Which boy, Sharon?'

Sharon pointed over at her mother. 'Ask her. She knows more about it than I do.'

Mrs Holmes jutted a hand in Sharon's direction. 'I will not have you talking to me like that! Is that clear?'

'Yes, Mum.' Almost too softly to be heard.

The arm jerked again. 'Is it?'

'Yes, Mum.'

Her father put down his cup and saucer. 'Sharon, who is this boy?'

Sharon looked at him wildly. 'There isn't any boy! There isn't any boy!' She screamed and hugged her knees up to her chest, burying her face between them.

'That's it,' said her mother. 'You cry. Get your father feeling sorry for you again.'

Sharon pulled her head away and glared: 'I'm not crying. I'm not . . . I'm not . . .'

She continued to stare at her mother, tears trickling from the corners of her eyes.

'Your mother only wanted to know who you've been seeing. If you've . . . if you're . . . involved in some way that's taking your mind off your work, we want to know about it, that's all.'

'Dad, there isn't any boy. I'm not going out with anybody.'

'You were, though, weren't you?' said Mrs Holmes.

'Yes! All right, yes, I was going out with someone and I'm not any more.'

'And who was he? Someone from school?'

Sharon sat forward onto the edge of the settee, then collapsed back again. 'Yes,' she answered quietly. 'His name's Mick Tracey and he's in the sixth form.'

Her mother's eyes flickered across the room. 'In that case, he ought to know better. I've a good mind to write a letter to the headmaster.'

'You can't!' Sharon was on her feet and shouting. 'You can't! Everyone'll laugh at me. You can't do that.' She pulled at her hair and twisted her head to one side. 'It doesn't . . . there isn't . . . I'm not going with him any more. I'm not, honest I'm not.'

Sharon stood there in the middle of the room, suddenly self-conscious.

Her mother grunted and opened the packet of cigarettes.

'All right,' her father said, 'No one's going to write a letter.'

Sharon crossed her arms, holding herself. Her mother struck a match and the flame startled upwards.

'I'm going upstairs,' said Sharon and left the room. Neither of her parents said anything.

There was a cat on the garage roof, grey and white, sitting on the corner like a statue. Sharon bit the inside of her lip. What right had they to go on at her like that? Moaning on and on, asking her questions as though it was some kind of interrogation. And . . . she put her hand to her face where her father had struck her. If only she lived with someone nice like her nan . . .

from *What About It, Sharon?* by John Harvey

* The discussion of Sharon's report becomes a family row. Whose fault is this?

* Look at what Sharon's mother says and does. What sort of mood is she in? How does she feel about Sharon? How does she feel about the way her husband handles the situation?

* Does Sharon deserve to be slapped? How does Mrs Holmes contribute to her husband's action?

* How does Sharon feel about her father in this extract:
  does she respect him
  is she frightened of him
  does she like him
  does she hate him?

* How could each member of the family have handled this situation better?

* Sharon is horrified when her mother suggests writing a letter to the headmaster. Should parents write to or visit school whenever they are worried about their children's progress, or should they not interfere?
  What advice would you give to parents who were worried about how their son or daughter was getting on at school?
  Should teachers get in touch with parents more often to share worries about pupils?

* In the last paragraph of this extract Sharon says about her parents, **'What right had they to go on at her like that?'** What rights do parents have in this sort of situation, do you think?

1. Improvise or write the scenes which might take place when Mr and Mrs Holmes meet some of Sharon's teachers at a parents' evening.

2. Write about a time when you had to discuss with your family how you were getting on at school. What happened?

3. A boy or girl arrives home from school with a school report in a sealed envelope. Write or improvise what happens when the envelope is opened by the parents.

What Do You Think?

Here is an extract from a survey carried out in a comprehensive school. About a hundred and fifty fifteen-year-olds were asked about their attitudes to school. In the extract below the results are all written down as a percentage of the total number of people asked.

What was your attitude to school when you were eleven years old?

very keen	17%
keen	12%
interested	29%
fairly interested	19%
not very interested	18%
hostile	5%

What is your attitude to school now?

very keen	3%
keen	21%
interested	25%
fairly interested	21%
not very interested	15%
hostile	15%

Do you think there is enough pressure on pupils to work at school?

too much	15%
about right	57%
not enough	28%

Do you think the range of subjects offered at school is wide enough?

yes	73%
no	27%

Do you think that you should only study at school subjects which might directly help your career later?

yes	48%
no	52%

How important do you think examinations are in your education?

vital	34%
fairly important	43%
not very important	14%
irrelevant	9%

* What would be your answers to these questions?

1. Perhaps working with a partner, plan a survey to find out what the people in your class think about some aspects of school. You might include questions on examinations, homework, choice of subjects, rules and routines such as assemblies, dinners, uniform . . . and so on.

Look at the extract from a survey above to help you to set out your questions.

A survey is a useful way of finding out what people think, but you do have to make sense of the results. When a magazine or a newspaper publishes the results of a survey it usually adds a report in which the writer picks out and perhaps comments on the results which seem most important to him or her.

In a report of this kind the figures in the survey are replaced by words and phrases like: **many, few, the majority, three-quarters, half.** If the report **does** quote the actual figures, they are written in words: eighty percent, not 80%. Here is part of the survey alongside part of a report on it:

It was reassuring to find that most pupils thought that there was enough pressure on them to work in school, but a few thought that there was too much and **it was disturbing** to discover that more than a quarter of the pupils thought that there was not enough pressure.

Do you think there is enough pressure on pupils to work at school?

too much	15%
about right	57%
not enough	28%

The writer of the report has expressed 57% as 'most pupils'; 15% as 'a few', and 28% as 'more than a quarter'. The writer has also added some opinions about the results and the words and phrases he uses to express these have been printed in bolder type.

Here is a longer extract from the report:

The survey showed that people's attitudes to school had changed since they were eleven years old. Sadly, many more pupils felt hostile towards school and fewer were very keen. However, happily, the majority were still interested in school and some had become more interested over the years.

It was reassuring to find that most pupils thought that there was enough pressure on them to work in school, but a few thought that there was too much and it was disturbing to discover that more than a quarter of the pupils thought that there was not enough pressure.

Perhaps surprisingly about three-quarters of the pupils thought that the range of subjects offered at school was wide enough. Half the pupils thought that only subjects which might help directly in careers should be offered.

Nearly eighty percent of the pupils thought, not surprisingly, that examinations were an important part of their education, but a significant minority—nine percent—thought that examinations were completely irrelevant.

Attitudes to homework were very mixed: a few of the pupils thought

2. Look through the report again and write down a list of the words and phrases in it which show the writer's **opinions**.

3. 15% of the pupils thought that there was too much pressure on them to work at school: the writer describes this number as 'a few'. 9% of the pupils thought that examinations were irrelevant: the writer describes this number as 'a significant minority'. What do these phrases tell you about the writer's views in each case, even though the views are not expressed directly?

4. Write a report of the results of your survey, including all the main points, drawing the reader's attention to the results which you think are most important and giving some of your opinions about the results.

Prison

At seventeen Ursula Brangwen is starting her first job – as an assistant teacher at a typical school in the early years of this century.

The latch of the door clicked, and they entered the big room. Ursula glanced down the place. Its rigid, long silence was official and chilling. Half way down was a glass partition, the doors of which were open. A clock ticked re-echoing, and Miss Harby's voice sounded double as she said:

'This is the big room – Standard Five-Six-and-Seven. – Here's your place – Five –'

She stood in the near end of the great room. There was a small high teacher's desk facing a squadron of long benches, two high windows in the wall opposite.

10   It was fascinating and horrible to Ursula. The curious, unliving light in the room changed her character. She thought it was the rainy morning. Then she looked up again, because of the horrid feeling of being shut in a rigid, inflexible air, away from all feeling of the ordinary day; and she noticed that the windows were of ribbed, suffused glass.

The prison was round her now! She looked at the walls, colour washed, pale green and chocolate, at the large windows with frowsy geraniums against the pale glass, at the long rows of desks, arranged in a squadron, and dread filled her. This was a new world, a new life, with which she was threatened. But still excited, she climbed into her chair at her teacher's

20   desk. It was high, and her feet could not reach the ground, but must rest on the step. Lifted up there, off the ground, she was in office. How queer, how queer it all was! How different it was from the mist of rain blowing over Cossethay. As she thought of her own village, a spasm of yearning crossed her, it seemed so far off, so lost to her . . .

Ursula faced her class, some fifty-five boys and girls who stood filling the ranks of the desks. She felt utterly non-existent. She had no place nor being there. She faced the block of children.

Down the room she heard the rapid firing of questions. She stood before her class not knowing what to do. She waited painfully. Her block of

30   children, fifty unknown faces, watched her, hostile, ready to jeer. She felt as if she were in torture over a fire of faces. And on every side she was naked to them. Of unutterable length and torture the seconds went by.

Then she gathered courage. She heard Mr Brunt asking questions in mental arithmetic. She stood near to her class, so that her voice need not be raised too much, and faltering, uncertain, she said:

'Seven hats at two-pence ha'penny each?'

A grin went over the faces of the class, seeing her commence. She was red and suffering. Then some hands shot up like blades, and she asked for the answer.

40   The day passed incredibly slowly. She never knew what to do, there came horrible gaps, when she was merely exposed to the children; and when, relying on some pert little girl for information, she had started a lesson, she did not know how to go on with it properly. The children were her masters. She deferred to them. She could always hear Mr Brunt. Like a machine, always in the same hard, high, inhuman voice he went on with his teaching, oblivious of everything. And before this inhuman number of children she was always at bay. She could not get away from it. There it was, this class of fifty collective children, depending on her for command, for command it hated and resented. It made her feel she could not breathe:
50   she must suffocate, it was so inhuman. They were so many, that they were not children. They were a squadron. She could not speak as she would to a child, because they were not individual children, they were a collective, inhuman thing . . .

The first week passed in a blind confusion. She did not know how to teach, and she felt she never would know. Mr Harby came down every now and then to her class, to see what she was doing. She felt so incompetent as he stood by, bullying and threatening, so unreal, that she wavered, became neutral and non-existent. But he stood there watching with that listening-genial smile of the eyes, that was really threatening; he said nothing, he made
60   her go on teaching, she felt she had no soul in her body. Then he went away, and his going was like a derision. The class was his class. She was a wavering substitute. He thrashed and bullied, he was hated. But he was master. Though she was gentle and always considerate of her class, yet they belonged to Mr Harby, and they did not belong to her . . .

Every now and again Mr Harby would swoop down to examine exercise books. For a whole hour, he would be going round the class, taking book after book, comparing page after page, whilst Ursula stood aside for all the remarks and fault-finding to be pointed at her through the scholars. It was true, since she had come, the composition books had grown more and more
70 untidy, disorderly, filthy. Mr Harby pointed to the pages done before her regime, and to those done after, and fell into a passion of rage. Many children he sent out to the front with their books. And after he had thoroughly gone through the silent and quivering class he caned the worst offenders well, in front of the others, thundering in real passion of anger and chagrin.

'Such a condition in a class, I can't believe it! It is simply disgraceful! I can't think how you have been let to get like it! Every Monday morning I shall come down and examine these books. So don't think that because there is nobody paying any attention to you, that you are free to unlearn
80 everything you have learned, and go back till you are not fit for Standard Three. I shall examine all books every Monday –'

Then in a rage, he went away with his cane, leaving Ursula to confront a pale, quivering class, whose childish faces were shut in blank resentment, fear, and bitterness, whose souls were full of anger and contempt of *her* rather than of the master, whose eyes looked at her with the cold, inhuman accusation of children. And she could hardly make mechanical words to speak to them. When she gave an order they obeyed with an insolent off-handedness, as if to say: 'As for you, do you think we would obey *you*, but for the master?' She sent the blubbering, caned boys to their seats,
90 knowing that they too jeered at her and her authority, holding her weakness responsible for what punishment had overtaken them. And she knew the whole position, so that even her horror of physical beating and

suffering sank to a deeper pain, and became a moral judgement upon her, worse than any hurt.

    She must, during the next week, watch over her books, and punish any fault. Her soul decided it coldly. Her personal desire was dead for that day at least. She must have nothing more of herself in the school. She was to be Standard Five teacher only. That was her duty. In school, she was nothing but Standard Five teacher. Ursula Brangwen must be excluded.

from *The Rainbow* by D. H. Lawrence

* The headmaster is in a rage; the pupils are resentful; Ursula is afraid. What has gone wrong?

* Whom do you have more sympathy for in this situation; Ursula or the children in her class? Why?

* What advice could you offer to Ursula and the children to try to improve the situation?

* What do you think hurts Ursula most:
    the headmaster's criticism of her
    his beating and bullying of the children
    the children's contempt for her
    the fact that she is forced to become less human in order to have
    any success with the class?
Is Ursula hurt by any other cause?

* Discipline in this school is obviously enforced mainly through fear and physical punishment. Are there other methods which could be used instead? Would any other methods help in this case?

1. Ursula is obviously very unhappy, but determined not to give in. Write a conversation in which a close friend or a relative tries to persuade Ursula to give up her teaching.

2. Suppose you are one of the children in Ursula's class. Say or write what happens to you during a typical day when she is in charge.

3. Write the report which Mr Harby might make to the school governors or the Education Authority on Ursula's progress as a teacher.

4. Write down what you think Mr Harby's views would be on what schools are for and how classes should be run. Say what you think of those views and why.

A Closer Look

1. 'It was fascinating and horrible to Ursula.'
What is there about the room that excites Ursula, and what repels her?

2. 'The prison was round her now!'
What makes Ursula think of the school as a prison?

3. 'they were not individual children, they were a collective, inhuman thing . . .'
Why do the children appear like this to Ursula? What other statements are made about the class that help to suggest that to Ursula they were a single, threatening mass?

4. What sort of teacher is Mr Brunt? What effect does it have on Ursula, do you think, that she can always hear Mr Brunt teaching his class next door?

5. Below are ten sentences from the extract. Explain what each one adds to your feelings about the school. What ideas or mental pictures does each one suggest to you?

In each sentence some words or phrases have been printed in bold type to help you.

    a. 'Its (the classroom's) **rigid, long silence** was **official and chilling.**' (line 2)
    b. 'Down the room she heard **the rapid firing** of questions.' (line 28)
    c. 'She felt as if she were **in torture over a fire of faces.**' (lines 30 to 31)
    d. 'Of **unutterable length** and **torture** the seconds went by.' (line 32)
    e. 'She was **red** and **suffering**. Then some hands shot up **like blades**, and she asked for the answer.' (lines 37 to 39)
    f. 'there came **horrible gaps**, when she was **merely exposed** to the children;' (lines 40 to 41)
    g. '**Like a machine**, always in the same **hard, high, inhuman** voice he went on with his teaching, oblivious of everything.' (lines 44 to 46)
    h. 'And before this **inhuman** number of children she was always **at bay.**' (lines 46 to 47)
    i. 'They were a **squadron.**' (line 51)
    j. 'Mr Harby would **swoop down** to examine exercise books.' (lines 65 to 66)

6. How can Mr Harby be 'bullying and threatening' even when he stands by and says nothing?

7. Is Mr Harby right to get angry about the children's work? Is he angry only because he thinks that the children are not making proper progress? Does Mr Harby's anger do any good? Does it do any harm?

8. 'She must have nothing more of herself in the school.' What does Ursula mean by this? What is the experience of teaching **doing** to her?

No more school in the afternoon

AFTERNOON lessons could be a thing of the past if a radical new plan for Oxfordshire secondary schools finds favour with parents.

County-wide consultations begin next month on a plan under which all formal classes would be crammed into the morning. Afternoons would be left open for children and adults living in the neighbourhood to undertake a whole range of activities, including music, games, drama, crafts, computer-training, community service, and typing.

If the scheme is accepted, it could be widely copied elsewhere. One school in Somerset has already run experiments along similar lines.

It is not designed to save money or to cut teachers' jobs. On the contrary, it will probably mean a longer day for staff and there is unlikely to be any extra money to back the change.

The consultations will be based on a discussion paper—to be issued in the next couple of weeks—which is understood to sketch three possible options.

The first is for formal school to run from 8.30 to 1.30 with lunch at the end of the morning. Children would then be free to go home; but schools would stay open during the afternoon for a whole range of club activities and projects in which adults would be encouraged to share.

The second option envisages that attendance in the afternoons would be compulsory but the activities would be similar to those under option one.

The third option would be to keep the traditional school day but to set aside occasional days or weeks for informal activities of this kind. This is already done by some schools in the county.

* Why do you think these proposals for changing the school day have been made? What would be gained by the changes? What would be lost?

* 'All formal classes would be crammed into the morning.' Which of the subjects that you study at school would be amongst these, do you think?

* What effect would it have on **you** if the 'informal' activities were not included in the 8.30 to 1.30 school day?

* What time would you have to get up in order to be at school by 8.30 a.m.? Would you mind this early start? Would it affect your life very much?

* Does it matter that children would be going to school in the dark for a longer part of the year than now?

* If options one or two were accepted, most children would be able to get home before dark in the winter. Is that important?

* Would the effects of the proposed changes on younger children be any different from the effects of the changes on older children?

* How would children whose parents are out at work all day be affected by the changes?

* Most school days at the moment are split into two sessions, none of which is longer than three or three and a half hours. If options one or two were accepted you would have to work for a five-hour session; with a break of (say) thirty minutes in the middle. Could you do this? How would you feel about it?

* What difficulties and advantages might there be in having adults sharing afternoon activities with pupils?

* Discuss the advantages and problems of each of the proposed systems and decide whether you would support option one, two or three, or leave things as they are now.

1. Oxfordshire parents were asked to comment on the proposed changes. Speaking as a parent **or** for yourself, write a letter to the Chairman of the Education Committee, clearly giving your reasons why you support **one** of the proposals; or why you wish the school system to remain as it is; or offering a new proposal of your own.

Writing a Business Letter

Sometimes you have to write a letter to someone you do not know, perhaps writing to a company to ask for information, or sending for details of something you have seen advertised in a magazine. Letters like this should always be efficient and polite (but not 'chatty' as a letter to a friend may be) and should be set out in one of the following ways:

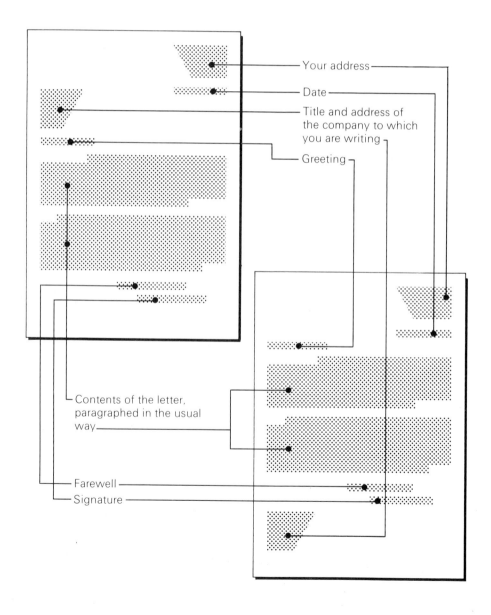

Your address

Date

Title and address of the company to which you are writing

Greeting

Contents of the letter, paragraphed in the usual way

Farewell

Signature

Here is an example of a business letter and its reply.

15, Chatsworth Road,

Maldern,

Warwickshire.

12th October 19—

The Arrow Bicycle Company,
Harston Industrial Estate,
Eversham.

Dear Sir or Madam,

I am rebuilding an old Arrow Bicycle which I found abandoned in a neighbour's shed. It needs a new gear-change lever and cable, but none of the local cycle shops has these parts and the newer ones, which are metric, do not fit.

The broken lever on the bicycle has the following words and numbers marked on it: Arrow Bicycles B/s 237. Do you still make these parts? If you do, can you tell me how much they cost and where I can buy them, please?

Yours faithfully,

Anne Chapman

Arrow Bicycle Company,
Harston Industrial Estate,
Eversham.

19th October 19--

Dear Miss Chapman,
              Thank you for your recent letter.
    You will be pleased to hear that we do still produce a small number of
the older type of lever and cable which you need. These parts are available
from a few specialist cycle shops in the country - the names and addresses of
which I have enclosed in this letter on a separate sheet. However, we can
also send the parts to you directly. The cost is £7.94 including VAT plus
£1.10 for postage and packing.
    Please let me know if you would like us to send you the replacement parts.

Yours sincerely,

JP.Martindale

Miss Anne Chapman,   Manager, Parts Supply Department.
15, Chatsworth Road,
Maldern,
Warwickshire.

1. Write Anne Chapman's second letter to the Arrow Bicycle
Company, in which she asks them to send her the parts for her bicycle
and encloses a Postal Order.

2. You want to stay on a camp site at Trehearne Farm, Lanston,
Cornwall for three days while on a cycling holiday with a friend during
the first week of August. Write a letter to the owner of the camp site
asking him or her to reserve a site for you.

3. Write a letter in response to one of the following advertisements:
    Old records in MINT condition! All the great stars and groups of
    the past 25 years at giveaway prices. Write for a full catalogue
    to — 'The Greats', Old Finsbury Road,
    Manchester M59 2RS.

    Riding . . . Sailing . . . Climbing . . . Canoeing . . . Wind Surfing . . .
    Are **you** ready for an adventure course? Send for details today
    to — 'Up and Away', Llanilan, North Wales. You'll be amazed at how
    cheap adventure can be!

    Stamps, coins, medals, badges . . .!
    We have probably the largest range of collectors' items in the
    country. Our latest catalogue is now available, price 50p. Please
    enclose a large stamped, addressed envelope. 'Set Pieces',
    29A Cranbrook Street, London, SE3.

THE LEWIS FAMILY

Our house

The Lewis family live in the house shown on page 53. The family moved into the house from a smaller one a few years ago. The house has four bedrooms, one of which has been divided into two by a partition wall. At the back of the house there is a small garden which is fairly private. Not much traffic uses the road in front of the house and the family car is normally parked there.

Here are some facts about the family:

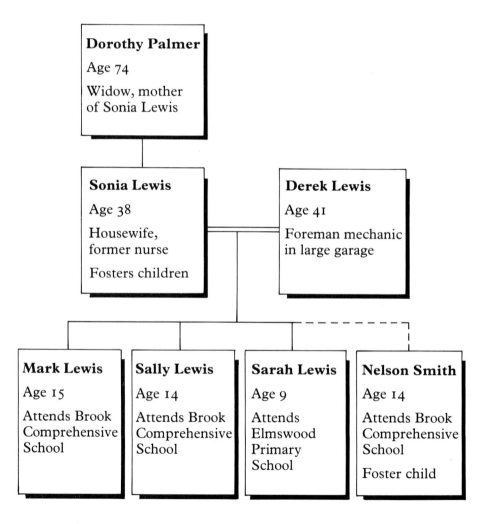

Dorothy Palmer

Age 74

Widow, mother of Sonia Lewis

Sonia Lewis

Age 38

Housewife, former nurse

Fosters children

Derek Lewis

Age 41

Foreman mechanic in large garage

Mark Lewis

Age 15

Attends Brook Comprehensive School

Sally Lewis

Age 14

Attends Brook Comprehensive School

Sarah Lewis

Age 9

Attends Elmswood Primary School

Nelson Smith

Age 14

Attends Brook Comprehensive School

Foster child

Dorothy Palmer, Sonia Lewis's mother, fell last year and broke her hip. As a result she gave up her home and came to live with the Lewises. After six months she left them to stay with her other daughter, Anne, and Anne's husband, Allan. Then Anne and Allan decided to emigrate to Canada . . .

Read the monologues below.

Mum in the park

Sonia Lewis

Really, we've been very lucky. Derek's got a good job which he likes and I enjoy the children. When I first gave up nursing I wasn't sure – that's years ago – but I'm glad now. I went back to nursing for a while when Sarah started school, but once we'd had this house for a few years and Derek got promoted, I didn't need to go on. So I stopped. I don't know now how I ever had the time . . . I wasn't fostering then, of course. I enjoy that, sharing the family with someone. You get all sorts, of course: we had a really rough child once, but Nelson's fine. He's settling in properly now – not quite so defensive – and he's good with Sarah. And Sally and Mark don't seem to mind. I wish Mark would take his school work a bit more seriously, like Sally, but there: you can't have everything . . . We're a happy family by and large, I think. We have our ups and downs, of course, like when Mum was here last, but by and large . . .

I thought Derek would make more fuss about Mother coming this time because things were not too good before she left after her last visit about a year ago. They don't fight: they just needle one another. He didn't say much, though, this time. It's more complicated as well, now, because Mother's slowed down a lot since she broke her hip last year and she'll need help. I suppose I *am* the one with the nurse's training, so I'm the obvious choice, but I did think it a bit much when my sister said she and Allan were emigrating. I mean, if I'd known they weren't going to be able to keep Mother I wouldn't have agreed to take another foster child . . . Nelson's got enough problems already with his mum in hospital, without feeling unwanted here. I suppose we could ask the authorities to find him another foster home, but he's been messed around enough already . . .

Dad at work

Derek Lewis

I like my work because it gives me responsibility and I like having to use my initiative. But I work a long day and I'm often worn out by the time I get home, and maybe I don't spend enough time with the family. I'm not really the worrying kind. I do get anxious, yes, and I went through a lot of worries when we got this house and the money was really tight, but I don't see the point in *looking* for troubles. Sonia's the same really, only she's better organised about some things than I am – around the house, anyway. I do my bit with the chores and so on, but I'm not really very interested in decorating and things. Mark's good at practical things – and he seems to be quite good on that guitar of his – but he never sticks at anything. And I dread his school reports. I get fed up with reading about how he could be good if he'd only try . . . I don't like to go on at him too much, but what he'll do for a job I *don't* know . . . Sally's doing well at school – she wants to stay on. I suppose – if that's what she really wants – we can afford it now. As long as we don't give in to Sarah about a horse! Not that we ever will. Even if we could afford it we'd have nowhere to keep it. She's potty about horses, that one.

You'd think three kids was enough, wouldn't you, without fostering others? I'd be happy with just the family; though Nelson's a nice boy, I must say, and Sonia gets a lot out of it. Mind you, the problems will start when Sonia's mother comes. I respect Dorothy, and I think it's our duty to take her in, but I can't in all honesty say that we get along too well. The kids resent her coming, I think, because someone will have to share a room. I tell them we must all make sacrifices . . . Anyway, two of the bedrooms are only separated by a hardboard wall so there isn't a great deal of privacy as it is . . .

Sarah Lewis

Got hay fever again. I always get rotten hay fever. It isn't fair. Sally never gets it, or Mark, or Dad. Mum does, but only sometimes.

Got another pony book from the library today. Just like the last one I got, *and* the one before that! Great! I love horses. I'm crazy about them. People go on and on at me about it, but I can't help it. I have this friend at school who's got one. Well, she *says* it's hers, anyway. I've seen her ride it: we went out to this place in her dad's car. It was great. But I haven't got a horse and I don't suppose I'll *ever* get one, really. All I've got is a brother and a sister. They're not as good as a horse, but Mark's all right. Sally's bossy, but Nelson – he's our extra – he sticks up for me *and* he plays with me. Mark thinks he's soft but he isn't. At least he doesn't blast out the house playing a stupid guitar all the time, or *boss* people! And he bought me a poster last week to put on my bedroom wall, of a Shetland pony. Now I maybe won't have anywhere to put it up because Gran's coming again, and this time it's *for ever* and I shall have to go in with Sally and all *she* wants is pop stars on the wall . . . It isn't fair. Just because I'm the youngest they think I don't *count*. It isn't fair . . .

Sarah   *Nelson doing his paper round*

Nelson Smith

It's all right here. I wish Mum was OK again. But this is not so bad, you know. Mark – he's OK. They're all OK. And Sarah – she's a cute little kid. Natural, you know. They're fair. And they don't make it obvious that I'm fostered. I was in another house before this. It was bad. They went on and on about how it didn't matter to them that I was black and that I was fostered. Didn't matter *hell*! But the Lewises are OK. There's a family down the street they know pretty well, the Kings – they're black, so it's

OK. Nobody worries. I worry sometimes. A lot. I worry about Mum. When she kept going crazy, having those breakdowns, she talked and talked. All about my dad and that and the accident. As if I was a friend or something, not like normal, you know, mother and son. I wish she was better. Sometimes it's as if I can't even remember what she looks like and it's the same with Dad, only worse. It's nice here, though. I like Mr Lewis, and Mrs Lewis, and that kid Sarah is great. She goes on and on about horses. I mean, *I* don't care about horses, but she's so – you know, so *full* of it – I like it. She's cute.

I'm sorry about the bedroom. It was great with a room of my own – I could be private and think to myself there. Now I'll have to share with Mark and he'll be mad; or else Sally and Sarah will have to share and Sally's always getting on to Sarah. Sometimes I think they don't like each other at all. I wish their gran wasn't coming . . .

Granny

Dorothy Palmer

I'm quite looking forward to going back to stay with Sonia again, although I realise I'll have to tread a bit more carefully with Derek than I did last time. I'm *not* difficult, whatever he thinks. He doesn't say much, but I can tell. He's a fine man and a good father and I don't want to be the cause of trouble. It's the last thing I want. But what's the alternative? Since I broke my hip I've slowed down a lot – I've got to admit it – and we're none of us getting any younger. I did hope I'd be staying with Anne and Allan but I suppose they were right to take this chance in Canada. I'm sure Allan would have been made redundant if he'd stayed here. And then again, Sonia does have the nursing experience, and that *does* matter when you're my age. It'll be a bit of a squeeze, I suppose, and I am sorry about the children having to share. I suppose the foster child could go somewhere else, but from what Sonia says he's had a lot to put up with. I don't want to be a burden, but everyone has responsibilities, haven't they?

I'll have to be very careful, though . . .

* What are the problems that face each member of the Lewis family, and what decisions does each one have to make?

You may prefer to work with a partner and write a list of the problems and decisions facing each member of the family, before discussing your ideas with the whole class.

1. The monologues of Sally and Mark Lewis have been left out. Write monologues for each of them showing their attitudes to other members of the family and their feelings about the problems they have to face.

2. Assume it is now six months later and Mrs Palmer has been living with the Lewises for most of that time.

Choose one of the following:

a. Write another series of monologues which tell the reader what has happened since Mrs Palmer's arrival, and how the members of the family feel now.

b. Show what happened in the family after the arrival of Mrs Palmer by writing a series of play scenes. These scenes might be like episodes in a radio or television serial, or they might make one complete play. Your play could include some monologues.

c. Write a story which describes what happened in the family after Mrs Palmer came to stay. You may choose to tell the story from the point of view of one of the members of the family.

The Nawahli Expedition

In November of last year an international expedition set out for the
Nawahli region of South America. The team of eight was led by Dr
Emmanuel Weber, the famous geologist and explorer. In recent years
there had been several earthquakes centred on the Nawahli region and
the main aim of the expedition was to investigate and measure the
source and extent of this earthquake activity.

In addition to Dr Weber the team included two other geologists: Dr
Pascale Raymond and Dr Emil Carr. Two botanists, Andrew Fildes and
Heidi Friedmann, also accompanied the expedition. The other three
members of the group were from British television and were hoping to

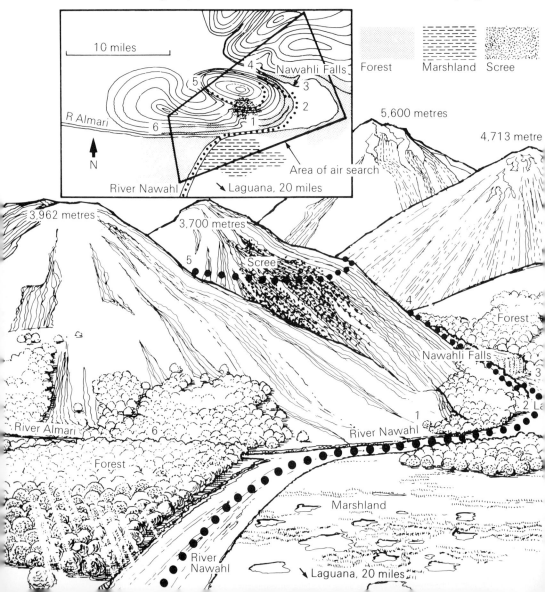

film the expedition. This television team included the well-known zoologist and broadcaster, Susan Crocker.

The expedition arrived at Laguana on November 11th and set off into the almost unknown and previously unexplored forests of the Nawahli region on December 1st. By December 10th the expedition had reached the confluence of the rivers Almari and Nawahl. It was soon after this that radio contact with the team was lost.

At first, this loss of contact did not disturb those at the Laguana base, but they became increasingly worried after a further ten days without any message, and a search was mounted by helicopter and on foot.

Despite intensive searches, almost no trace was found of the group and — after five weeks without contact — hope of finding any member of the expedition alive was abandoned.

Then, Martina Seboda, a television sound engineer with the expedition, was discovered in a distressed state in a makeshift shelter seventeen miles outside the area of the search. She was without food and was delirious.

Mrs Seboda was suffering from malnutrition, exhaustion and a broken arm which she had tried unsuccessfully to set herself. She was flown immediately to hospital and slowly began to recover. Relatives and colleagues of the lost group waited anxiously at the hospital for Mrs Seboda to recover sufficiently to tell them the story of the ill-fated expedition . . .

A few quick questions

* How many people were in the expedition party?
* What were their names and jobs?
* How long did it take the expedition to reach the place where the rivers Almari and Nawahl join?
* How many days passed between the loss of radio contact with the expedition and the beginning of the search?
* How long did the search go on for?
* What injuries had Mrs Seboda suffered?

1. Tell Mrs Seboda's story.
The map shows the area which was to be explored by the expedition, and also the area covered by the search parties. The route shown on the map was sketched in by Mrs Seboda, and she also added the numbers, **which refer to important events which happened on the journey.**

Mrs Seboda's story could take the form of an interview which has been recorded and then written out later, or it could be her own written account.

Colons to introduce lists: revision ⬤

⬤

A colon introduces a list; it announces that a list of things is about to be presented. For example:

> I went to an international farm camp this summer. There were young people from everywhere there: Japanese, Americans, Jamaicans, Germans, a Mexican boy, and many more.

Punctuate the following lists correctly:

1. By the time Anita was fourteen she had attended seven schools one in Germany two in Hong Kong one in the Falklands and three in England

2. The severe winter brought havoc to our garden and killed many plants the peonies the veronica two lovely broom bushes and the lilac tree

3. When we came to check the camping equipment at the beginning of the summer term all we found were the following three tents four groundsheets a bag of guy ropes and two mallets

4. Upon investigation by the police the burglar's bag was found to contain one jemmy a stocking six silver candlesticks a hammer and a roll of sticky tape

5. The first five books in my library were these *Winnie the Pooh Home Fun The Beano Annual The Highway Code* and a Littlewood's shopping catalogue

The colon also introduces a list in a notice. Here is an example:

> The following third year pupils should see the Year Tutor at 1.20 today in his room:
>
> D. Peters
> N. Mukhopadia
> J. Hargreaves
> C. Harrison
> C. Rhodes

Note that when a list is displayed as a column, you do not need a comma between each item.

Punctuate the following, setting them out as ordinary lists or as notices:

1. The Film Society hopes to show films of this sort westerns comedies musicals cartoons science fiction

2. The bus will call at the following places in the city centre General Post Office The Pier City Hall The Railway Station The Bus Station

3. The usual tourist route for foreign visitors to Britain includes London Oxford Stratford upon Avon York Edinburgh

4. It is surprising how many versions there are of the name Elizabeth Liz Lisa Libby Beth Betty Bess

5. During the second world war many provincial cities in Great Britain were bombed including Plymouth Coventry Belfast Portsmouth Hull and Glasgow

Semi-colons in a list: revision

In the notice below commas are already used in some of the items:-

> The talent contest includes the following acts:
>> a juggler, who claims to be able to keep at least six objects in the air at one time
>> a singer who recently appeared in an opera in Milan
>> two stunt women, the *Incredible Belles*
>> a new seven-piece rock band, including three singers

If this notice were written out as a list, using commas to separate each item, the list would be rather confusing, so you separate each item by using a **stronger** punctuation mark, the semi-colon. The list would now read:

> The talent contest includes the following acts: a juggler, who claims to be able to keep at least six objects in the air at one time; a singer who recently appeared in an opera in Milan; two stunt women, the *Incredible Belles*, and a new seven-piece rock band, including three singers.

Note that the final **and** now has a comma in front of it to show that it is not part of the previous item.

1. Rewrite the notice below as a list, using semi-colons correctly:

Some of Eleanor Fox's most successful works also published by Seville Books include:
The Last Chance, an exciting adventure story
Angel Despair, a powerful romantic novel
The End of the Line, a story of conflicting passions during the last war, set in Clapham
No Way, a fast-moving story about life with a travelling fair

Some lists or notices contain several **groups** of things. For example:

The clothes displayed in the shop window included:
three pairs of jeans, in assorted colours and styles
two pairs of boots, two pairs of high-heeled shoes and one pair of sandals
two dresses — one yellow and one blue
two tee-shirts — one patterned
one V-neck pullover, one polo-neck pullover and one sleeveless cardigan

In this list each **group** should be separated from the next by a semi-colon:

The clothes displayed in the shop window included: three pairs of jeans, in assorted colours and styles; two pairs of boots, two pairs of high-heeled shoes and one pair of sandals; two dresses — one yellow and one blue; two tee-shirts — one patterned, and one V-neck pullover, one polo-neck pullover and one sleeveless cardigan.

2. Write out the list below, using semi-colons correctly:

When Uncle Sid looked carefully into the 'box of assorted household articles' which he had bought at the auction, he found some surprises: an electric toaster dating from 1938 six teaspoons six knives and one fork a *Beano Annual* for 1946 four hideous glass dishes and the broken remains of an electric clock.

3. Write a similar list using semi-colons correctly, describing the contents of another 'box of assorted household articles' bought at an auction.

Writing a Radio Play

Here is an extract from a play intended for the stage.

	(A room in a stately home. The room is dimly lit by light coming in from outside through a window. A man and woman enter. The man looks round and then moves to turn on the light. The woman speaks.)
Woman:	No. Wait a minute. (She crosses to the window and closes the curtains. The man turns on the light. They both look round the room, which is lavishly furnished with antiques and has many pictures on the walls.)
Man:	Quite a collection.
Woman:	Come on, let's get on with it.
Man:	Right. (He puts down a small bag he is carrying, opens it, and takes out a small knife.) Which one is it, then?
Woman:	What?
Man:	(looking round at the pictures) Which one is it we're supposed to be taking?
Woman:	Oh. It's the Van Gogh.
Man:	Right. (He looks vaguely at the pictures.) The Van Gock.
Woman:	Gogh, idiot! Like 'cough'.
Man:	(offended) All right.
	(pause)
Woman:	Well, go on then; let's get started.
Man:	O.K. Get it off the wall and turn it over.
Woman:	Me? Oh . . . er . . . (She moves towards one of the pictures, then turns and moves towards another, then stops.) I'm not sure . . . I, er . . .
Man:	(horrified) I don't believe it!
Woman:	I thought *you* knew.
Man:	Me? I'm just the cutter.
Woman:	The what?
Man:	Cutter. Like 'nutter'.
	(We hear the sound of footsteps from off-stage.)
Woman:	Sh! What was that?
	(They listen. We hear the sound of a door closing. The man rushes across and turns out the light; the woman opens the curtains. They look around, frightened, and then hide hurriedly behind a table.) Look! (She points to the door, the handle of which is slowly turning.)

If you want to record this play for radio, there are several problems to think about.

1. The listeners cannot see the man and woman enter the room.
2. The listeners may not realise that the curtains have been closed and the light turned on. The line 'Wait a minute' will not make sense.
3. The listeners do not know that the room has many pictures in it and is full of antiques.
4. The listeners do not know that the man pulls a knife out of his bag.
5. The listeners cannot *see* the woman trying to decide which picture is the Van Gogh.
6. The listeners do not know that the two thieves have turned off the light, opened the curtains and hidden behind a table.
7. The listeners cannot see the door handle turning at the end.

* How could you solve these problems? When you have worked out some possible solutions, look at the passage below and see how the writer tried to adapt the play for radio. Compare his ideas with yours. Which are more sensible? Would both ideas – yours and his – work equally well? Which solutions make fewer changes in the script?

	(We hear the sound of quiet but echoing footsteps in a large house. Then we hear the sound of a door being opened cautiously. It creaks slightly. We hear a man's voice.)
Man:	(whispering) It's a bit dark. I'll put the light on.
Woman:	No. Wait a minute. I'll close the curtains. (We hear the woman crossing the room and drawing the curtains.) There.
Man:	Right. (We hear the click of a light switch. Pause.) Quite a collection.
Woman:	There's a lot of good stuff here: antique.
Man:	And all those pictures.
Woman:	Come on, let's get on with it.
Man:	Right. (We hear the sound of a bag being placed on the floor and opened.) I'll just get my knife. (slight pause) Right. Which one is it, then?
Woman:	What?
Man:	Which picture is it we're supposed to be taking?
Woman:	Oh. It's the Van Gogh.
Man:	Right. (pause) Er . . . um. The Van Gock.
Woman:	Gogh, idiot! Like 'cough'.
Man:	(offended) All right. (pause)

Woman:	Well, go on then; let's get started.
Man:	O.K. Get it off the wall and turn it over. (During the following the woman's voice moves away and back again.)
Woman:	Me? Oh . . . er . . . Yes, it must be this . . . No, of course, it's this one . . . er . . . I'm not sure . . . I, er . . .
Man:	(horrified) I don't believe it!
Woman:	I thought *you* knew.
Man:	Me? I'm just the cutter.
Woman:	The what?
Man:	Cutter. Like 'nutter'. (We hear the sound of footsteps at a distance.)
Woman:	Sh! What was that? (Pause. We hear the sound of a door closing.) Quick, the light! I'll open the curtains. (We hear the sounds of hurried movement, the click of the light switch and the swish of the curtains being opened.)
Man:	Now what?
Woman:	Hide. Here, behind this table. (We hear the sounds of hurried movement. Pause.) Look!
Man:	What?
Woman:	The door handle. It's turning. Someone's coming in.
Man:	(quietly) Help!

1. Here are the next few lines from the same stage play. First decide what the problems will be for listeners, and then re-write the extract for radio.

	(The door opens slowly. Enter a figure dressed in dark clothing. It looks about the room, crosses to the curtains, closes them and then turns on the light. It is a man. He does not see the other two. He carries a small bag. He opens the bag and takes out a knife. He goes across to one of the pictures and takes it down from the wall. He begins to open the back of the picture with his knife. The first man gets up from behind the table and moves behind the second man. He is still carrying his knife.)
Man:	Excuse me.
Second Man:	(dropping his knife to the floor) Aagh!
Man:	I want to ask you a question.
Second Man:	(turning) Don't kill me, guv! I never –
Man:	I was wondering if you could tell us which of these pictures is the Van Gock?

2. Write a play for radio.

Making Definitions

In the game called *Animal, Vegetable, Mineral*, person A thinks of an object which person B has to discover by asking A no more than twenty questions about the object. B may only ask questions which can be answered **Yes** or **No**. A gives B some help before B starts to ask his questions. He tells B whether the object is animal, vegetable or mineral, or a mixture.

    Animal includes all living creatures which can move and feel, or once-living creatures.

    Vegetable includes all growing things, or objects made from once-growing things.

    Mineral includes water, stone, plastics, metals and all objects made from them.

Here is an example of the game being played:

A: The object is animal.

B: Is it human?	A: Yes.
B: Is it alive?	A: Yes.
B: Is it male?	A: No.
B: Is it one particular person?	A: Yes.
B: Is she famous?	A: Yes.
B: Is she rich?	A: Yes.
B: Is she powerful?	A: Yes.
B: Is she a member of the Royal Family?	A: Yes.
B: Is it the Queen?	A: Yes!

To start the game **A** has divided all possible objects in the world into three groups or **categories**. He has then told **B** that the object is animal. Therefore, **B** can forget about all vegetable and mineral objects and concentrate on animal only: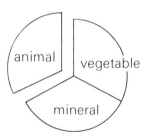

From this point on, see how **B**'s next few questions narrow down the possible objects:

Here is another example of the game being played:

A: The object is mineral and vegetable.

B: Is it man-made?	A: Yes.
B: Is the mineral contained in it water?	A: No.
B: Is the mineral stone?	A: Partly, yes.
B: Is it a building of some kind?	A: Yes.
B: Is it a large building?	A: No.
B: Do people live in this building?	A: No.
B: Are vehicles of any kind kept in it?	A: No.
B: Is it used by the public?	A: Yes.
B: Do you have to pay to enter it?	A: No.
B: Does it contain any furniture?	A: No.
B: Does it contain any equipment?	A: Yes.
B: Is it something to do with communications?	A: Yes.
B: Is it a telephone box?	A: Yes!

With a partner, play the game until both of you become expert at finding the object.

The questioner (B) in *Animal, Vegetable, Mineral* first tries to find the main category to which the unknown object belongs. He then discovers what the unknown object is by finding out step by step what makes it different from others in the same main category. Objects can be **defined** in a similar way:

object	main category to which it belongs	differences between this object and others in the same main category
telephone box	building	it is small it contains a telephone it is for public use
kangaroo	marsupial	lives in Australia has very long hind legs can leap with great power

So, using this plan, you can now write the definitions:

> A telephone box is a small building which contains a telephone for public use.
> A kangaroo is a marsupial which lives in Australia, has very large hind legs and can leap with great power.

Using this plan define the following:

1. a shirt
2. an electric kettle
3. a wrist watch
4. a supermarket
5. a ten pence piece
6. a submarine
7. a bicycle
8. a theatre
9. an ostrich
10. a sandwich
11. a disco
12. a television
13. a roller skate
14. a bruise
15. midnight
16. a sigh
17. a ghost
18. a spring
19. an aeroplane
20. a river

Slogans

Many advertisements try to grab your attention by using a slogan. Here are some examples:

> Drinka pinta milka day.
> Milk has gotta lotta bottle.
> You'll never put a better bit o' butter on your knife.
> My goodness, my Guinness!
> A Mars a day helps you work, rest and play.
> Have a break, have a Kit Kat.
> Go to work on an egg.
> Think once, think twice, think bike.
> Clunk, click, every trip.
> It beats, as it sweeps, as it cleans.
> Beanz means Heinz.
> Philips, simply years ahead.

An effective slogan is usually short and has to be 'catchy'. There are many ways of making it catchy. Some of the methods include:

1. repetition of words: **Think** once, **think** twice, **think** bike.

Which of the slogans in the list above use repetition?

2. alliteration: — gotta lotta bottle
   Clunk, click —

How much alliteration can you find in the slogans?

3. rhyme: A Mars a **day** helps your work, rest and **play**.
   half-rhyme: It b**eats**, as it sw**eeps** as it cl**eans**.

How many of the slogans use rhyme and half-rhyme to make their effect?

4. rhythm: **Drinka pinta milka day**.

Which slogans make their effect through rhythm?

5. jokes and plays on words: **Go to work on an egg**.

How many meanings can you work out for this slogan?

1. Think of other advertising slogans you know. Write them down and try to work out what it is that makes them catchy.

2. Try to make up slogans for these products or campaigns:

   Betty Simpson cakemix
   Castaway milk chocolate bar
   Crystal double-glazing for houses
   Clean — a household soap
   Arrow — a high-performance sports car
   Senorita — a perfume
   Start! — a soft cola drink
   a campaign to persuade cyclists to have good lights on their bicycles
   a campaign to discourage parents from carrying children in the front seat of a car
   an anti-litter campaign.

GHOSTS

The Unseen Housemate

A shuffling step across the upper floor,
Loose-fitting slippers flapping down the stair,
The handle turns and stealthily the door
Swings on its hinges, and there's no-one there –
No-one my eyes can see; but, happen, he
Who dwelt here ere I came had keener sight –
At least I wonder what he saw the night
He hanged himself from the old apple-tree.

Wilfrid Gibson

A Night at a Cottage

On the evening that I am considering I passed by some ten or twenty cosy barns and sheds without finding one to my liking: for Worcestershire lanes are devious and muddy, and it was nearly dark when I found an empty cottage set back from the road in a little bedraggled garden. There had been heavier rain earlier in the day, and the straggling fruit trees still wept over it.

But the roof looked sound, there seemed no reason why it should not be fairly dry inside – as dry, at any rate, as I was likely to find anywhere.

I decided: and with a long look up the road, and a long look down the road, I drew an iron bar from the lining of my coat and forced the door, which was only held by a padlock and two staples. Inside, the darkness was damp and heavy: I struck a match, and with its haloed light I saw the black mouth of a passage somewhere ahead of me: and then it spluttered out. So I closed the door carefully, though I had little reason to fear passers-by at such a dismal hour in so remote a lane: and lighting another match, I crept down this passage to a little room at the far end, where the air was a bit clearer, for all that the window was boarded across. Moreover, there was a little rusted stove in this room: and thinking it too dark for any to see the smoke, I ripped up part of the wainscot with my knife, and soon was boiling my tea over a bright, small fire, and drying some of the day's rain out of my steamy clothes. Presently I piled the stove with wood to its top bar, and setting my boots where they would best dry, I stretched my body out to sleep.

I cannot have slept very long, for when I woke the fire was still burning brightly. It is not easy to sleep for long together on the level boards of a floor, for the limbs grow numb, and any movement wakes. I turned over, and was about to go again to sleep when I started to hear steps in the passage. As I have said, the window was boarded, and there was no other door from the little room – no cupboard even – in which to hide. It occurred to me rather grimly that there was nothing to do but to sit up and face the music, and that would probably mean being hauled back to Worcester jail, which I had left two bare days before, and where, for various reasons, I had no anxiety to be seen again.

The stranger did not hurry himself, but presently walked slowly down the passage, attracted by the light of the fire: and when he came in he did not seem to notice me where I lay huddled in a corner, but walked straight over to the stove and warmed his hands at it. He was dripping wet: wetter than I should have thought it possible for a man to get, even on such a rainy night; and his clothes were old and worn. The water dripped from them onto the floor: he wore no hat, and the straight hair over his eyes dripped water that sizzled spitefully on the embers.

It occurred to me at once that he was no lawful citizen, but another wanderer like myself; a gentleman of the Road; so I gave him some sort of greeting, and we were presently in conversation. He complained much of the cold and the wet, and huddled himself over the fire, his teeth chattering and his face an ill white.

'No,' I said, 'it is no decent weather for the Road, this. But I wonder this cottage isn't more frequented, for it's a tidy little bit of a cottage.'

Outside the pale dead sunflowers and giant weeds stirred in the rain.

50 'Time was,' he answered, 'there wasn't a tighter little cot in the co-anty, nor a purtier garden. A regular little parlour, she was. But now no folk'll live in it, and there's very few tramps will stop here either.'

There was none of the rags and tins and broken food about that you find in a place where many beggars are used to stay.

'Why's that?' I asked.

He gave a very troubled sigh before answering.

'Gho-asts,' he said; 'gho-asts. Him that lived here. It is a mighty sad tale, and I'll not tell it you: but the upshot of it was that he drowned himself, down to the mill-pond. All slimy, he was, and floating, when they
60 pulled him out of it. There are fo-aks have seen un floating on the pond, and fo-aks have seen un set round the corner of the school, waiting for his childer. Seems as if he had forgotten, like, how they were all gone dead, and the why he drowned hisself. But there are some say he walks up and down this cottage, up and down; like when the smallpox had 'em, and they couldn't sleep but if they heard his feet going up and down by their do-ars. Drownded hisself down to the pond, he did; and now he Walks.'

The stranger sighed again, and I could hear the water squelch in his boots as he moved himself.

'But it doesn't do for the likes of us to get superstitious,' I answered. 'It
70 wouldn't do for us to get seeing ghosts, or many's the wet night we'd be lying in the roadway.'

'No,' he said; 'no, it wouldn't do at all. I never had belief in Walks myself.'

I laughed.

'Nor I that,' I said. 'I never see ghosts, whoever may.'

He looked at me again in his queer melancholy fashion.

'No,' he said, ' 'Spect you don't ever. Some folk do-ant. It's hard enough for poor fellows to have no money to their lodging, apart from gho-asts sceering them.'

80 'It's the coppers, not spooks, make my sleep uneasy,' said I. 'What with coppers, and meddlesome-minded folk, it isn't easy to get a night's rest nowadays.'

The water was still oozing from his clothes all about the floor, and a dank smell went up from him.

'God! man,' I cried, 'can't you NEVER get dry?'

'Dry?' He made a little coughing laughter, 'Dry? I shan't never be dry

. . . 'tisn't the likes of us that ever get dry, be it wet OR fine, winter OR summer. See that.'

90   He thrust his muddy hands up to the wrist in the fire, glowering over it fiercely and madly. But I caught up my two boots and ran crying out into the night.

by Richard Hughes

* Tell some ghost stories you know, perhaps about places near where you live. Experiment with different tones of voice to help fix your listeners' attention. How can you use the tone of your voice to build up suspense and a spooky atmosphere?

1. Write a ghost story. Try to build up an eerie atmosphere, as Richard Hughes did, by describing important details about the place and the events in your story.

Try to find an ending which will startle or satisfy your readers, or leave them wondering . . . Perhaps the ending might be written as just one sentence in a paragraph of its own.

Below are some suggestions for your story.

a. A footfall in an empty house . . . the branch of a tree scratching against a window pane . . . a white face peering in at a window from the darkness outside . . . a shape on the stair behind you . . . Write a story which will frighten your reader.

b. Schools during the day are bustling and fairly noisy places. At night they are dark, quiet and deserted. Suppose you have been locked in, accidentally, on the second floor overnight . . . What happens?

c. The local guide book mentions the ghost of Sir James Hawkes which is said to haunt Exton Hall each year on the anniversary of his strange and untimely death. It all sounds quite normal, even cosy. What the guide book does not mention, because it had not been revealed at the time it was written, is that this seemingly cosy ghost appears to have changed its nature. There have been some strange and rather sinister events in Exton recently . . .

d. 'I'll believe it when I see it,' she said, and to do her justice, she **did** believe it when she did see it less than twelve hours later . . .

A Closer Look

1. Why do you think Richard Hughes wrote this story as if someone was telling it?

2. How do the words 'devious', 'muddy', 'bedraggled' and 'straggling' (lines 3 to 5) help to create an atmosphere?

3. What impression do you get of the inside of the cottage from phrases like: the 'darkness was damp and heavy'; 'its haloed light'; 'the black mouth of a passage'; 'spluttered out' (lines 11 to 13)?

4. Notice the number of times that water and wetness are mentioned in describing the stranger between lines 34 and 41. How does this prepare you for the end of the story? Does it spoil the ending?

5. 'Outside the pale dead sunflowers and giant weeds stirred in the rain.' This description (line 49) draws the reader's attention from the inside to the outside of the cottage for a moment, rather like a change of camera shot in a film. Why does the writer do this, do you think? What effect does it have? What connection is there between this picture or image of the dead flowers and giant weeds and the story?

6. Look back through the story from line 50 and note the number of times that the second tramp hints that there are ghosts in the cottage. Why do you think Richard Hughes allows us to realise who the second tramp is before the storyteller does? Once you know that the second tramp is a ghost, does that make the rest of the story more or less enjoyable?

The Brown Lady of Raynham Hall

On 19 September 1936 Mr Indra Shira and his assistant, Captain Provand, were taking photographs of various parts of Raynham Hall, in Norfolk. In the afternoon they set up their equipment to photograph the main staircase. Captain Provand took a flash-light exposure and was preparing the camera to take another when Mr Shira saw, he said later, a luminous but transparent figure gliding down the stairs towards him. He called out to his colleague and pressed the exposure trigger. When the photograph was processed a cloudy shape resembling a woman dressed in a long, flowing gown appeared on the print. Expert examination found nothing to suggest tampering at any stage. Here is the photograph:

* What questions would you want to ask Mr Shira and Captain Provand to convince yourself that this was a genuine photograph of an actual ghost?

Haunting face fails to halt colliery

By Malcolm Pithers

THE NATIONAL Coal Board said yesterday that production at a South Yorkshire colliery would continue, despite a miner's reported sighting of a ghost underground.

Mr Stephen Dimbleby, aged 23, fled from the coal-face at Silverwood colliery, near Rotherham, after seeing what he described as a faceless figure wearing an old-fashioned helmet.

Yesterday the Coal Board said that as far as they were concerned Mr Dimbleby was an extremely reliable worker.

NCB officials have agreed to move Mr Dimbleby from the coal face to the coal preparation section of the pit, with a £50 a week reduction in his wages.

A Coal Board officer said yesterday that Mr Dimbleby had reported seeing the figure of a miner which had no eyes, no nose or mouth.

It was also said to be wearing a waistcoat and a grubby shirt. Modern miners wear bright orange overalls.

Understandably in the circumstances Mr Dimbleby simply dropped his equipment and ran out of the walkway towards the pit shaft. He ran for a mile and a half, and was crying and shaking when a pit deputy stopped him.

Mr Dimbleby was then taken to Rotherham district hospital and treated for shock.

The NCB press office in Doncaster has discovered that a miner was killed in a coal-face accident 14 years ago, near the spot where Mr Dimbleby saw the apparition.

1. Make a list of facts which support what Mr Dimbleby said had happened down the mine.

2. If the last paragraph of this article had been left out, would it have made much difference to your belief in the ghost? Why?

3. Mr Dimbleby said that the ghost had no eyes, nose or mouth. Does that make you more or less convinced about his story?

4. How can you tell that Mr Dimbleby was genuinely frightened by what happened?

5. Write the account which Mr Dimbleby might give to the Coal Board about what happened and about why he wishes to change his job.

6. Suppose someone who lived in your area saw a faceless figure at his or her place of work. Either write the story of what happened or, with a partner, improvise an interview between a reporter and the witness. The reporter should make a written note of the main points of the witness's story — including what happened, where and when it happened and who was involved — and of any statements he or she might want to print in full in the newspaper. Then, **from the reporter's notes,** work together to write the newspaper story.

From
The Guardian
19 March 1982

Poltergeist

John Randall was eighteen years old in July 1910 when his work as a carpenter took him to Enniscorthy, a town in County Wexford, Ireland. He lived as a lodger in a house with five other people: a labourer called Nicholas Redmond and his wife; two other lodgers – George Sinnott and Richard Roche – and a servant girl called Bridget Thorpe. Here is part of John Randall's account of some of the incidents which took place in the house.

On Saturday, the 2nd of July, 1910, I came to work in Enniscorthy as an improver in the carpentry trade. Monday, I went to lodge in a house in Court Street. There were two other men stopping in the same house as lodgers. They slept in the same room also, but shared a different bed at the other side of the room. My bed was in a recess in the wall at the opposite side. There was one large window in the room, which opened both top and bottom. The room was about fourteen feet square and ten feet high. There was one door opening into it. The window described was in the back wall of the house nearly opposite the door opening into the room from the top landing. There were two other doors on the same landing opening into different rooms. There was also a fireplace in the room.

On Monday night, July 4th, we went to bed, and my first night in the strange house I think I slept pretty soundly. We got up at six o'clock the next morning and went to work. We left off work at six in the evening, and went to bed the same time as the night before, between 10 and 10.30 o'clock, slept soundly, and all went well, also on Wednesday.

Went to bed on Thursday night at 10.45, the three of us going as before. We blew out the light, but the room was then fairly lightsome. We had only been about ten minutes in bed when I felt the clothes being gently drawn from my bed. I first thought that it was the others that were playing a joke, so I called out, 'Stop, George, it's too cold.' Then I heard them say, 'It's Nick' (that is the name of the man of the house). It wasn't any of them that had pulled the clothes off me, so they thought it was Nick that was in the room, and did not mind.

At this time the clothes had gone off my bed completely, and I shouted to them to strike a match. When they struck a match, I found that my bedclothes were at the window. The most curious part was that the same time when the clothes were leaving my bed, their bed was moving. I brought back the clothes and got into bed again. The light was then put out, and it wasn't long until we heard some hammering in the room – tap-tap-tap-like. This lasted for a few minutes, getting quicker and quicker. When it got very quick their bed started to move out across the floor, and that made us very frightened, and what made us more frightened was the door being shut, and nobody could open it without making a great noise.

They then struck a match and got a lamp. We searched the room thoroughly, and could find nobody. Nobody had come in the door. We called the man of the house; he came into the room, saw the bed, and told us to push it back and get into bed (he thought all the time one of us was playing a trick on the other). I said I wouldn't stay in the other bed by myself, so I got in with the others; we put out the light again, and it had been only a couple of minutes out when the bed ran out on the floor with the three of us. Richard struck a match again, and this time we all got up and put on our clothes; we had got a terrible fright and couldn't stick it any longer. We told the man of the house we would sit up in the room until daylight. During the time we were sitting in the room we could hear footsteps leaving the kitchen and coming up the stairs; it would stop on the landing outside the door and wouldn't come into the room. The footsteps and noises continued through the house until daybreak . . .

. . . The following Friday night it was very bad. The bed turned up on one side, and threw us out on the floor, and before we were thrown out, the pillow was taken from under my head three times. When the bed rose up, it fell back without making any noise. This bed was so heavy, it took both the woman and the girl to pull it out from the wall without anybody in it, and there was only three castors on it. After being thrown out of the big bed, the three of us got into my bed. We were not long in it when it started to rise, but could not get out of the recess it was in unless it was taken to pieces. It ceased about daybreak, and that finished that night's performance.

It kept very bad then for a few nights. So Mr Murphy, from the *Guardian* office, and another man named Devereux, came and stopped in the room one night. They sat on two chairs in the room, while we (John Randall and George Sinnott – Richard Roche had left) lay each in our own beds. We were not long in bed when I felt a terrible feeling over me like a big weight. I then felt myself being taken from the bed, but could feel no hands, nor could I resist going. All I could say was: 'I'm going, I'm going: they're at me!' I lay on the floor in a terrible state, and hardly able to speak. The perspiration was pouring through me. They put me back in bed again, and nothing more than strange knockings and noises happened between that and morning. We slept again in the room the next night, but nothing serious happened. We then got another lodging, and the people (the Redmonds and Bridget Thorpe) left it also. For the three weeks I was in the house I lost nearly three-quarters of a stone weight. I never believed in ghosts until that, and I think it would convince the bravest man in Ireland.

from *Vol. 25* of the *Proceedings of the Society for Psychical Research*

* Why does John Randall describe the bedroom so fully in the first paragraph? Try to draw a plan of the room and landing.

* Does the description of what happened on Thursday and Friday nights strike you as funny, or is it frightening, or both? Is John Randall **trying** to make it sound funny?

* Do you think you would have done the same things as John Randall did if you had been in the same situation? Why?

1. Write an account of the events John Randall describes from the point of view of one of the other people in the house at the time. Your account may include details which you make up, but it must also fit the facts and events which John Randall describes.

2. Mr Murphy from *The Guardian* will want to write an article about this for his newspaper. Some people are bound to suggest that the events described in the article were made up or imagined, so he will want to interview all the people who were in the house before he decides what to write.

In a small group improvise or write some of these interviews. Then each of you write the article for the newspaper. Compare your version with those of others in the group. Which is the most convincing account?

3. Take one of the episodes in John Randall's account and use it as the starting point for a play. You should decide before you begin whether your play is intended to frighten the audience, or to make them laugh. Decide also whether you want the play to be for the stage or for radio.

Family's poltergeist exorcised by priest

By a Correspondent

POLICE called a priest to a Coventry house yesterday to conduct an exorcism after a six-hour rampage by a poltergeist.

A series of upheavals caused chaos in the quiet home of Paul and Marion Haigh. Crockery was smashed, a TV over-turned and an oil heater propelled across the floor.

'I have never seen anything like it,' said Chief Inspector Graham Pinder of Coventry police.

The couple had called police to their home in Monk Road, to see for themselves what was happening.

'A kitchen dresser toppled over in front of my eyes,' said PC Ian Coates. 'It would normally have taken two men to shift that, and I really have no explanation.'

The attacks began for the couple, their daughter Karen, aged 17, and their foster boy, Ian, aged eight, at 5 am.

'I heard the dog barking but got up to go to work as normal,' said Mr Haigh who is a window cleaner. 'It was unusual because he is normally a quiet dog, but he shot out of the house and did not come back.'

Mrs Haigh watched petrified as furniture flew across the lounge and ornaments crashed to the floor. She said, 'I heard something smash and when I rushed into the room my table flew around the room and a biscuit tin whizzed past my head and crashed in the corner. I was petrified.'

Dr Cyril Bardey, aged 90, a priest who has worked all over the world, performed the exorcism in the lounge.

He said the Lord's Prayer and called to the spirits of evil to depart from the room. 'There has been something evil in this house that has fed on fear but now it has gone.' Dr Bardey said.

Haunted family quits home

THE family whose home in Coventry has been the subject of a series of ghostly attacks have left the house.

More crockery was smashed and furniture was again overturned on Saturday as poltergeist activity continued at the house in Monk Road, where police were called after the first attack on Friday and a constable saw a kitchen dresser fall over.

Social workers were in the house on Saturday morning when a second incident occurred, and it was after the third later in the day that two mediums held a seance and advised the family to leave for four or five days.

Mr Paul Haigh, his wife Marion, aged 56, daughter 17, and foster son Ian, eight, moved out on Saturday night and were yesterday seeking bed and breakfast accommodation through the council.

Mr Haigh said: 'The mediums told us a spiritual playmate of Ian caused the damage.'

Poltergeist threatens foster child

Mr and Mrs Paul Haigh whose house was disrupted at the weekend by a series of incidents in which furniture and other belongings were flung around the house, say that eight-year old Ian was unconcerned by the incidents, which terrified them and two police officers who witnessed some of the havoc.

A medium called to the house claimed that the spirit was that of a 23-year-old crippled drug addict who died two years ago and who had come back as a nine year old boy. Another medium called from a local Spiritualist church said it was a nine-year-old boy called John. For the past two years Ian has been holding conversations with an imaginary playmate called John.

Ian is now staying with the Haigh's married daughter, and there has been no repetition of the incidents at the house.

Mr Haigh said yesterday:

'With Ian in the house things start to happen. We don't blame him—it's the spirit that's got hold of him. He is becoming too strong and boisterous for my wife to handle.'

adapted from *The Guardian*, 15, 17, 22 August, 1981

* From the way they are used in these newspaper articles, what would you say is the meaning of these words: exorcism, medium, séance?

* Compare the statements made by the two mediums. Which do you find the more convincing, or do you find both explanations unlikely?

* Look at the two accounts of poltergeist activity in this chapter. What similarities are there between them? What important differences are there between them?

1. From the evidence of the two accounts on the previous pages, try to explain what a poltergeist seems to be. Your explanation should include: what a poltergeist does; the effects it seems to have on people and on animals; what might cause it.
     Your explanation might begin:
     A poltergeist is a force which . . .

* Here is one definition of a poltergeist:
A poltergeist is generally believed to be a force which is set in motion by the mental energy released by someone who is very upset or disturbed, especially a teenager.
How far does this theory help explain the events in either of the cases of poltergeist activity recounted in this chapter?

Certainty

At the time when his brother Wilfred was killed at the end of the First World War, Harold Owen was away at sea . . .

We were lying off Victoria. I had gone down to my cabin thinking to write some letters. I drew aside the door curtain and stepped inside and to my amazement I saw Wilfred sitting in my chair. I felt shock run through me with appalling force and with it I could feel the blood draining away from my face. I did not rush towards him but walked jerkily into the cabin – all my limbs stiff and slow to respond. I did not sit down but looking at him I spoke quietly: 'Wilfred, how did you get here?' He did not rise and I saw that he was involuntarily immobile,[1] but his eyes which had never left mine were alive with the familiar look of trying to make me understand; when I spoke his whole face broke into his sweetest and most endearing dark smile. I felt no fear – I had not when I first drew my door curtain and saw him there; only exquisite[2] mental pleasure at thus beholding[3] him. All I was conscious of was a sensation of enormous shock and profound astonishment that he should be here in my cabin. I spoke again. 'Wilfred dear, how can you be here, it's just not possible . . .' But still he did not speak but only smiled his most gentle smile. This not speaking did not now as it had done at first seem strange or even unnatural; it was not only in some inexplicable way perfectly natural but radiated a quality which made his presence with me undeniably right and in no way out of the ordinary. I loved having him there: I could not, and did not want to try to understand how he had got there. I was content to accept him, that he was here with me was sufficient. I could not question anything, the meeting in itself was complete and strangely perfect. He was in uniform and I remember thinking how out of place the khaki looked amongst the cabin furnishings. With this thought I must have turned my eyes away from him; when I looked back my cabin chair was empty . . .

I felt the blood run slowly back to my face and looseness into my limbs and with these an overpowering sense of emptiness and absolute loss . . . I wondered if I had been dreaming but looking down I saw that I was still standing. Suddenly I felt terribly tired and moving to my bunk I lay down; instantly I went into a deep oblivious[4] sleep. When I woke up I knew with absolute certainty that Wilfred was dead.

[1]*not able to move*　　　　　　from *Journey from Obscurity* by Harold Owen
[2]*extreme*
[3]*seeing*
[4]*forgetful, unaware*

* Was this a ghost? What possible alternative explanation could you give to Harold Owen for what happened?

* Do you think what Harold Owen saw is better described as a ghost or as a vision?

* We usually associate ghosts with darkness and an eerie atmosphere. What is there about Harold Owen's account of **his** experience which makes it quite different from 'usual' stories about ghosts?

* Does Harold Owen try to frighten his reader in this piece?

* What are the physical effects on Harold Owen of seeing his brother? What does he **think** and **feel** about seeing him there? What are his feelings after his brother has disappeared?

* What physical action and mental thought might have made the ghost or vision disappear when it did?

1. How can you tell that Harold Owen was very fond of his brother? Write down words or phrases which show this.

2. Write a suitable alternative title for this piece.

3. In what ways is this extract from an autobiography like a complete short story? Look particularly at the ending of the piece, especially at the last sentence.

Miller's End

When we moved to Miller's End,
   Every afternoon at four
A thin shadow of a shade
   Quavered through the garden-door.

Dressed in black from top to toe
   And a veil about her head
To us all it seemed as though
   She came walking from the dead.

With a basket on her arm
   Through the hedge-gap she would pass,
Never a mark that we could spy
   On the flagstones or the grass.

When we told the garden-boy
   How we saw the phantom glide,
With a grin his face was bright
   As the pool he stood beside.

'That's no ghost-walk,' Billy said,
   'Nor a ghost you fear to stop –
Only old Miss Wickerby
   On a short cut to the shop.'

So next day we lay in wait,
   Passed a civil time of day,
Said how pleased we were she came
   Daily down our garden-way.

Suddenly her cheek it paled,
   Turned, as quick, from ice to flame,
'Tell me,' said Miss Wickerby.
   'Who spoke of me, and my name?'

'Bill the garden-boy.'
             She sighed,
   Said, 'Of course, you could not know
How he drowned – that very pool,
   A frozen winter – long ago.'

Charles Causley

Shades of Meaning

The words you choose to describe people or things often show what you feel about them and may persuade other people to share your views. Words which show or produce feelings in this way are called **emotive** words. Emotive words may suggest **positive** feelings about a person or thing, or they may suggest **negative** ones. For example, here are two people describing the same person:

Carol: Oh yes, I've known him for years, he's a stocky, well-built man, with an imposing nose; he's a determined, impressive sort of person.

Ben: Oh yes, I know him all right, he's a stunted, podgy man, with a monstrous nose; he's a stubborn, bullying sort of person.

Carol likes this person. She uses **positive** adjectives to describe him: **stocky, well-built, imposing, determined, impressive.**

Ben, however, obviously dislikes this person. He uses **negative** adjectives to describe him: **stunted, podgy, monstrous, stubborn, bullying.**

A third person, Andrea, has no strong feelings about this person. She describes him like this:

Andrea: Oh yes, I know who you mean, he's a short, fat man, with a large nose; he seems a firm, dominant sort of character to me.

Andrea uses **neutral** adjectives: **short, fat, large, firm, dominant.**

1. Below is a collection of twenty neutral, or unemotive adjectives which might be used to describe people. Each one has been placed in the centre of a group of emotive adjectives with similar meanings. Write down each neutral adjective and then decide which of the other words in each group are positive, and which are negative. Whether a word is neutral or positive or negative is sometimes open to argument, and you may find it useful to discuss your views. You may also find a dictionary useful. Here is an example of how you might set out this work:

positive	neutral	negative
stocky, compact	short	squat, stunted

compact	squat	petite	puny
short		**small**	
stunted	stocky	tiny	undersized

plump	well-built	easy-going	lax
fat		**tolerant**	
gross	podgy	indulgent	mild

infantile	youthful	gargantuan	grand
young		**large**	
immature	junior	imposing	monstrous

towering	overgrown	spirited	fiery
tall		**quick-tempered**	
lanky	lofty	irritable	snappy

tender-hearted	gushing	commanding	overbearing
emotional		**dominant**	
sentimental	warm	impressive	bullying

feeble	delicate	muscle-bound	robust
weak		**strong**	
frail	wishy-washy	brawny	powerful

gaunt	slim	unyielding	stubborn
thin		**firm**	
skinny	lean	determined	steadfast

venerable doddering **old** senile elderly	matey oily **friendly** warm-hearted familiar
unassuming aloof **reserved** cold modest	dull tranquil **calm** apathetic serene
wild enthusiastic **excitable** spontaneous rash	confidential reticent **private** sly furtive

2. Write descriptions of three imaginary people in which you describe the first in a neutral way, the second in a positive way and the third in a negative way.

3. Write two descriptions of another imaginary person: one in which you describe the person in an unemotive, neutral way; the other in which you describe him or her in an emotive way — negatively or positively.

FACE TO FACE

Ishi

The story of Ishi begins for us in California early in the morning of the twenty-ninth day of August in the year 1911 and in the corral of a slaughter house. It begins with the sharp barking of dogs which roused the sleeping butchers. In the dawn light they saw a man at bay, crouching against the corral fence – Ishi.

They called off the dogs. Then, in some considerable excitement, they telephoned the sheriff in Oroville two or three miles away to say that they were holding a wild man and would he please come and take him off their hands. Sheriff and deputies arrived shortly, approaching the corral with guns at the ready. The wild man made no move to resist capture, quietly allowing himself to be handcuffed.

The sheriff, J. B. Webber, saw that the man was an Indian, and that he was at the limit of exhaustion and fear. He could learn nothing further, since his prisoner understood no English. Not knowing what to do with him, he motioned the Indian into the wagon with himself and his deputies, drove him to the county jail in Oroville, and locked him up in the cell for the insane. There, Sheriff Webber reasoned, while he tried to discover something more about his captive he could at least protect him from the excited curiosity of the townspeople and the outsiders who were already pouring in from miles around to see the wild man.

The wild man was emaciated to starvation, his hair was burned off close to his head, he was naked except for a ragged scrap of ancient covered-wagon canvas which he wore around his shoulders like a poncho. He was a man of middle height, the long bones, painfully apparent, were straight, strong, and not heavy, the skin colour somewhat paler in tone than the full copper characteristic of most Indians. The black eyes were wary and guarded now, but were set wide in a broad face, the mouth was generous and agreeably moulded.

It should be said that the sheriff's action in locking Ishi up was neither stupid nor brutal given the circumstances. Until Sheriff Webber took the unwonted measure of keeping them out by force people filled the jail to gaze through the bars of his cell at the captive. Later, Ishi spoke with some diffidence of this, his first contact with white men. He said that he was put up in a fine house where he was kindly treated and well fed by a big chief. That he would eat nothing and drink nothing during his first days of captivity Ishi did not say. Such was the case; nor did he allow himself to sleep at first. Quite possibly it was a time of such strain and terror that he suppressed all memory of it. Or he may have felt that it was unkind to recall his suspicions which proved in the event groundless, for Ishi expected in those first days to be put to death. He knew of white men only that they were the murderers of his own people. It was natural that he should expect, once in their power, to be shot or hanged or killed by poisoning.

Meanwhile, local Indians and half-breeds as well as Mexicans and Spaniards tried to talk to the prisoner in Maidu, Wintu, and Spanish. Ishi listened patiently but uncomprehendingly, and when he spoke it was in a tongue which meant no more to the Indians than to the whites.

An anthropologist, Professor Waterman, of the University of California, hurried out to meet Ishi. Professor Waterman had spent many years studying the lives and languages of the Indians of Northern and of Central Yana Territory, and had learned a little of their language. Perhaps Ishi was of the southernmost tribe of Yana, believed to be extinct. Waterman had learned some of the vocabulary of the Northern and Central Yana from two old Indians: Batwi and Chidaimiya.

With a copy of Batwi's and Chidaimiya's vocabularies in his pocket, Waterman arrived in Oroville where he identified himself to Sheriff Webber and was taken to visit the wild man. Waterman found a weary, badgered Indian sitting in his cell, wearing the butcher's apron he had been given at the slaughter house, courteously making what answer he could in his own language to a barrage of questions thrown at him in English, Spanish, and assorted Indian from a miscellaneous set of visitors.

Waterman sat down beside Ishi, and with his phonetically transcribed list of Northern and Central Yana words before him, began to read from it, repeating each word, pronouncing it as well as he knew how. Ishi was attentive but unresponding until, discouragingly far down the list, Waterman said *siwini* which means yellow pine, at the same time tapping the pine framework of the bed on which they sat. Recognition lighted up the Indian's face. Waterman said the magic word again; Ishi repeated it

after him, correcting his pronunciation, and for the next moments the two of them banged at the wood of the bed, telling each other over and over, *siwini, siwini*!

With the difficult first sound recognition achieved, others followed. Ishi was indeed one of the lost tribe, a Yahi; in other words, he was from the southernmost Yana. Waterman was learning that the unknown Yahi dialect differed considerably but not to the point of unintelligibility from the two northern ones of his list. Together he and Ishi tried out more and more words and phrases: they were beginning to communicate. After a while Ishi ventured to ask Waterman, *I ne ma Yahi*? 'Are you an Indian?' Waterman answered that he was. The hunted look left Ishi's eyes – here was a friend. He knew as well as did his friend that Waterman was not an Indian. The question was a tentative and subtle way of reassuring and being reassured, not an easy thing to do when the meaningful shared sounds are few . . .

The ordeal of civilisation began for Ishi at the door of the Oroville jail. It was a sunny September morning less than a week after he had strayed out of his own Stone Age Yahi world into a twentieth century world.

Fearful and preoccupied with the new reality, Ishi started down Main Street . . .

Side by side, Ishi and Waterman walked from the jail to the railroad station. Women and children peered discreetly from windows or over picket fences to catch a glimpse of the Wild Man, and there were several men and older boys waiting on the platform to see him. They kept their distance, and they were quiet. There was probably a little fear mixed with curiosity in their quietness. Ishi was by way of becoming a hero to them, a

man of myth and mystery to whom tales cling and grow. He remains so to this day.

The black face of the white man's Demon rushed toward the platform, pouring out clouds of sparks and smoke, and filling the ears with its hollow, moaning voice. Mill Creek and Deer Creek were within range of the sound of that voice; twice a day Ishi had heard it ever since he could remember, and he had watched the train hundreds of times as it snaked along below him, bellowing and belching. His mother had reassured him as a small boy when he was afraid of it, telling him that it was a Demon who followed white men wherever they went, but that Indians need have no fear of it; it never bothered them.

Today, Ishi wondered. He had not been so near it before; it was larger and noisier and speedier than he had realised. Would the Demon know that he was Indian? He was wearing white men's clothes, and his hair was short like theirs. It might be as well to watch from a little distance, from the shelter of a tree or bush, as he was accustomed to, at least until he had made sure that his friend was correct in his assurance that the Demon always stayed in its own old tracks, and that it carried people safely from place to place. He stepped behind a cottonwood tree alongside the platform. The Demon drew up beside the station and came to a halt. Ishi saw that it was as his friend had said – it did not leave its tracks. The white men who should have the most reason to be afraid, showed no signs of uneasiness, rather they climbed in and out of it, and one of them sat in its head, waving to those below. Ishi came back onto the platform, and made no objection to going aboard with Waterman. He had committed himself too far to turn back, nor did he wish to do so; where his new friend led he would follow.

During the trip, Ishi sat very quiet. He found the speed of the train exciting; also the view through the window of hills and fields and houses racing in and out of sight. He averted his eyes from the strangers in the car, blotting out their nearness by not looking directly at them. The Demon carried them rapidly down its old tracks and after some hours onto a ferry boat which took them, engine, cars, and passengers, across Carquinez Straits. He was sorry to leave the train at the Oakland Mole, but ahead lay further wonders – another ferry trip, this time across the bay to San Francisco; and after that, a long ride in a trolley car to the Museum of Anthropology.

Arrived at the museum, Ishi had gone a longer way than the miles which separated him from Deer Creek canyon. It was eleven o'clock in the evening of Labor Day, September 4, 1911, when Ishi the Yahi completed a trip out of the Stone Age into the clang and glare of the Iron Age – a place of clocks and hours and a calendar; of money and labour and pay; of government and authority; of newspapers and business. Now he, too, was a modern man, a city dweller with a street address.

from *Ishi in Two Worlds* by Theodora Kroeber

* Why do you think so many people poured into Oroville to see what they called 'The wild man'? What did they hope to find?

* Two definitions of wild are:
    a. being in a state of nature; not tamed or cultivated
    b. crazy, violent.
Does either of these definitions fit the description of Ishi and the way he behaves? Is 'Wild man' a suitable name for Ishi?

* Ishi later referred to the jail in which he was held as 'a fine house'. What does this tell you about his life before his capture?

* Why did Ishi expect to be killed at first? Why didn't the white men kill him as he had expected?

* Can you understand why the two men, Ishi and Waterman, were so excited when Ishi recognised the word, *'siwini'*?

* What problems do you think Ishi and his helpers, like Professor Waterman, would have had to face during the months following his discovery? What might Ishi have found remarkable and frightening about twentieth century life?

* 'The ordeal of civilisation began for Ishi at the door of the Oroville jail.' An ordeal is a severe trial or test. How can civilisation with all its modern comforts and welfare be an ordeal?

* What aspects of your modern life would you wish to show to and share with a person like Ishi? What things would he be better off without? What advantages might Ishi—with his 'uncivilised' way of life—have to offer us?

* At first Ishi is very afraid of the railway train but he eventually reasons that it is safe to climb aboard. How does he convince himself that it will be safe to do so?

1. Look at the three photographs of Ishi on pages 94 and 95. Write about the feelings or impressions you get of his character from his face and appearance. Do you get the same feelings from each picture?

2. How would a primitive person see your world: the place where you live and what you do? Imagine a primitive person were to change places with you for a few weeks. Write his or her account of life in your world. What do you think **your** problems would be if you lived in his or her world?

Snake

A snake came to my water-trough
On a hot, hot day, and I in pyjamas for the heat,
To drink there.
In the deep, strange-scented shade of the great dark carob-tree
I came down the steps with my pitcher
And must wait, must stand and wait,
                                for there he was at the trough before me.

He reached down from a fissure in the earth-wall in the gloom
And trailed his yellow-brown slackness soft-bellied down,
                        over the edge of the stone trough
And rested his throat upon the stone bottom,
And where the water had dripped from the tap,
                                in a small clearness,
He sipped with his straight mouth,
Softly drank through his straight gums,
                                into his slack long body.
Silently.

Someone was before me at my water-trough,
And I, like a second comer, waiting.

He lifted his head from his drinking, as cattle do,
And looked at me vaguely, as drinking cattle do,
And flickered his two-forked tongue from his lips,
                                and mused a moment,
And stooped and drank a little more,
Being earth-brown,
                earth-golden from the burning bowels of the earth

On the day of Sicilian July, with Etna smoking.
The voice of my education said to me
He must be killed,
For in Sicily the black, black snakes are innocent,
                                the gold are venomous.

And voices in me said, *If you were a man*
You would take a stick and break him now,
                                and finish him off.

But must I confess how I liked him,
How glad I was he had come like a guest in quiet,
                                to drink at my water-trough
And depart peaceful, pacified, and thankless,
Into the burning bowels of this earth.

Was it cowardice, that I dared not kill him?
Was it perversity, that I longed to talk to him?
Was it humility, to feel so honoured?
I felt so honoured.

And yet those voices:
If you were not afraid, you would kill him!

And truly I was afraid, I was most afraid,
But even so, honoured still more
That he should seek my hospitality
From out the dark door of the secret earth.

He drank enough
And lifted his head, dreamily, as one who has drunken,
And flickered his tongue like a forked night on the air, black,

Seeming to lick his lips,
And looked around like a god, unseeing, into the air,
And slowly turned his head,
And slowly, very slowly, as if thrice adream,
Proceeded to draw his slow length curving round
And climb again the broken bank of my wall-face.

And as he put his head into that dreadful hole,
And as he slowly drew up, snake-easing his shoulders,
                              and entered farther,
A sort of horror, a sort of protest
            against his withdrawing into that horrid black hole,
Deliberately going into the blackness,
                      and slowly drawing himself after,
Overcame me now his back was turned.

I looked round, I put down my pitcher,
I picked up a clumsy log
And threw it at the water-trough with a clatter.
I think it did not hit him,
But suddenly that part of him that was left behind
                      convulsed in undignified haste,
Writhed like lightning, and was gone
Into the black hole, the earth-lipped fissure in the wall-front,
At which, in the intense still noon, I stared with fascination.

And immediately I regretted it.
I thought how paltry, how vulgar, what a mean act!
I despised myself
and the voices of my accursed human education.

And I thought of the albatross,
And I wished he would come back, my snake.
For he seemed to me again like a king,
Like a king in exile, uncrowned in the underworld,
Now due to be crowned again.

And so, I missed my chance with one of the lords
Of life.
And I have something to expiate;
A pettiness.

D. H. Lawrence

* What do you think of the way the man acted? Discuss these views.

   He should not have interfered with the snake in case it bit him, but
   he should have told others about it so that it could be destroyed
   later.
   He should have driven the snake off without hurting it: why
   should he wait for a snake?
   He should have left the snake alone and been patient: it was a
   beautiful creature and deserved respect.
   He should have killed the snake at once and thought no more
   about it.

* What does D. H. Lawrence mean by 'the voice of my education'?

* Why does he call his education 'accursed'?

* Why does the man attack the snake when it is retreating?

   Is it because he is afraid of it?
   Is it to prove that he is not afraid?
   Is it because of the 'voices'?
   Is it because he likes the snake and does not want it to leave?
   Is it because he hates the idea of the creature returning to
   darkness?
   Or is it for some other reason?

* D. H. Lawrence often repeats words and phrases — for example:
   'And must wait, must stand and wait'
and 'He sipped with his straight mouth,
    Softly drank through his straight gums'
What other examples of this sort of repetition can you find? What
effect do they have?

* Is *Snake* a poem? Try to explain the reasons for your views.

Is there any creature for which you feel an instinctive respect?

1. Write about your feelings.

2. Write a story or poem in which someone comes face to face with
such a creature.

Car Fights Cat

In a London crescent curving vast
A cat sat—
Between two rows of molar houses
With birdsky in each grinning gap.
Cat small—coal and snow
Road wide—a zone of tar set hard and fast
With four-wheeled speedboats cutting
A dash
      for it from
            time to time.

King Cat stalked warily midstream
As if silence were no warning on this silent road
Where even a man would certainly have crossed
With hands in pockets and been whistling.

The cat heard it, but royalty and indolence
Weighed its paws to pitboots
Held it from the dragon's-teeth of safety first and
   last,
Until some Daimler hurrying from work
Caused cat to stop and wonder where it came
   from—
Instead of zig-zag scattering to hide itself.

Maybe a deaf malevolence descended
And cat thought car would pass in front—
So spun and walked all fur and confidence
Into the dreadful tyre treads. . . .
A wheel caught hold of it and
FEARSOME THUDS
Sounded from the night-time of black axles in
UNEQUAL FIGHT
That stopped the heart to hear it.

But cat shot out with limbs still solid,
Bolted—spitting fire and gravel
At an unjust God who built such massive
Cat-proof motorcars in His graven image,
Its mind made up to lose and therefore win
By winging towards the wisdom toothgaps of the
    canyon houses,
LEGS AND BRAINS INTACT.

                    Alan Sillitoe

* What **exactly** happens? Discuss this until you are satisfied with your account of the events in the poem.

* Why do you think the poem is called *Car Fights Cat* and not *Cat Fights Car*?

* Did the poem end as you expected? If it did, **why** did you expect it to end this way? If it did not, what **did** you expect to happen, and why?

* How can you tell that Alan Sillitoe wants us to share the cat's view of things?

1. Write a poem or story in which something weak clashes with something stronger, but survives. Here are some ideas which might help you:

    a fish caught in a net
    a pilot flying an aeroplane through a storm
    a plant or tree growing in very hostile surroundings
    a canoeist caught in rapids
    an animal trapped in a field which is being harvested.

Lok

Lok is a primitive man, living thousands of years ago. He is watching another man, a stranger, from some trees at the side of a river . . .

The bushes twitched again. Lok steadied by the trees and gazed. A head and a chest faced him, half-hidden. There were white bone things behind the leaves and hair. The man had white bone things above his eyes and under the mouth so that his face was longer than a face should be. The man turned sideways in the bushes and looked at Lok along his shoulder. A stick rose upright and there was a lump of bone in the middle. Lok peered at the stick and the lump of bone and the small eyes in the bone things over the face. Suddenly Lok understood that the man was holding the stick out to him but neither he nor Lok could reach across the river . . . The stick began to grow shorter at both ends. Then it shot out to full length again.

The dead tree by Lok's ear acquired a voice.

'Clop!'

His ears twitched and he turned to the tree. By his face there had grown a twig: a twig that smelt of other, and of goose, and of the bitter berries that Lok's stomach told him he must not eat. This twig had a white bone at the end. There were hooks in the bone and sticky brown stuff hung in the crooks. His nose examined this stuff and did not like it. He smelled along the shaft of the twig. The leaves on the twig were red feathers and reminded him of goose. He was lost in a generalised astonishment and excitement.

from *The Inheritors* by William Golding

* What has happened? Describe what has taken place as clearly as you can.

* Suggest words which would have helped Lok to describe and understand what happened. Why hasn't he got these words?

* Lok uses his sense of smell to investigate the 'twig'. Why isn't he satisfied with just seeing? Why doesn't he pick it up or touch it?

* The obvious thing for Lok to do is to shelter or run away. Why doesn't he do this?

* Lok has already learned from his previous experiences that he must not eat the bitter berries as they are bad for his stomach. What do you think he is likely to learn from this new experience?

1. Write a description of someone coming up against something which is a completely new experience. It might be a small child coming across something which an older person would understand, or an adult coming across a very advanced piece of technology, or someone who has no knowledge of modern technology—aeroplanes, radio, television, modern weapons and so on—finding an example of one of these.

Invasion from Mars

A series of what appeared to be explosions on Mars have been observed from Earth. Later a 'thing' is found on Horsell common . . .

The Thing lay almost entirely buried in sand, amidst the scattered splinters of a fir tree it had shivered to fragments in its descent. The uncovered part had the appearance of a huge cylinder, caked over, and its outline softened by a thick, scaly, dun-coloured incrustation. It had a diameter of about thirty yards.

★   ★   ★

When I returned to the common the sun was setting. Scattered groups were hurrying from the direction of Woking, and one or two persons were returning. The crowd about the pit had increased, and stood out black against the lemon-yellow of the sky – a couple of hundred people, perhaps. There were a number of voices raised, and some sort of struggle appeared to be going on about the pit. Strange imaginings passed through my mind. As I drew nearer I heard Stent's voice:

'Keep back! Keep back!'

A boy came running towards me.

'It's a movin',' he said to me as he passed – 'a-screwin' and a-screwin' out. I don't like it. I'm a-goin' 'ome, I am.'

I went on to the crowd. There were really, I should think, two or three hundred people elbowing and jostling one another, the one or two ladies there being by no means the least active.

'He's fallen in the pit!' cried someone.

'Keep back!' said several.

The crowd swayed a little, and I elbowed my way through. Everyone seemed greatly excited. I heard a peculiar humming sound from the pit.

I saw a young man, a shop assistant in Woking I believe he was, standing on the cylinder and trying to scramble out of the hole again. The crowd had pushed him in.

The end of the cylinder was being screwed out from within. Nearly two feet of shining screw projected. Somebody blundered against me, and I narrowly missed being pitched on to the top of the screw. I turned, and as I did so the screw must have come out, and the lid of the cylinder fell upon the gravel with a ringing concussion. I stuck my elbow into the person behind me and turned my head towards the Thing again. For a moment that circular cavity seemed perfectly black. I had the sunset in my eyes.

I think everyone expected to see a man emerge – possibly something a little unlike us terrestrial men, but in all essentials a man. I know I did. But, looking, I presently saw something stirring within the shadow – greyish billowy movements, one above another, and then two

luminous discs like eyes. Then something resembling a little grey snake, about the thickness of a walking-stick, coiled up out of the writhing middle, and wriggled in the air towards me – and then another.

A sudden chill came over me. There was a loud shriek from a woman behind. I half turned, keeping my eyes fixed upon the cylinder still, from which other tentacles were now projecting, and began pushing my way back from the edge of the pit. I saw astonishment giving place to horror on the faces of the people about me. I heard inarticulate exclamations on all sides. There was a general movement backward. I saw the shopman struggling still on the edge of the pit. I found myself alone, and saw the people on the other side of the pit running off, Stent among them. I looked again at the cylinder, and ungovernable terror gripped me. I stood petrified and staring.

A big greyish, rounded bulk, the size perhaps, of a bear, was rising slowly and painfully out of the cylinder. As it bulged up and caught the light, it glistened like wet leather. Two large dark-coloured eyes were regarding me steadfastly. It was rounded, and had, one might say, a face. There was a mouth under the eyes, the lipless brim of which quivered and panted, and dropped saliva. The body heaved and pulsated convulsively. A lank tentacular appendage gripped the edge of the cylinder, another swayed in the air.

Those who have never seen a living Martian can scarcely imagine the strange horror of their appearance. The peculiar V-shaped mouth with its pointed upper lip, the absence of brow ridges, the absence of a chin beneath the wedge-like lower lip, the incessant quivering of this mouth, the Gorgon groups of tentacles, the tumultuous breathing of the lungs in a strange atmosphere, the evident heaviness and painfulness of movement, due to the greater gravitational energy of the earth – above all, the extraordinary intensity of the immense eyes – culminated in an effect akin to nausea. There was something fungoid in the oily brown skin, something in the clumsy deliberation of their tedious movements unspeakably terrible. Even at this first encounter, this first glimpse, I was overcome with disgust and dread.

Suddenly the monster vanished. It had toppled over the brim of the cylinder and fallen into the pit, with a thud like the fall of a great mass of leather. I heard it give a peculiar thick cry, and forthwith another of these creatures appeared in the deep shadow of the aperture.

At that my rigour of terror passed away. I turned and, running madly, made for the first group of trees, perhaps a hundred yards away; but I ran slantingly and stumbling, for I could not avert my face from these things.

There, among some young pine trees and furze bushes, I stopped, panting, and waited further developments. The common round the sand-pits was dotted with people, standing, like myself, in a half-fascinated terror, staring at these creatures, or, rather, at the heaped gravel at the edge of the pit in which they lay. And then, with a renewed horror, I saw a round, black object bobbing up and down on the edge of the pit. It was the head of the shopman who had fallen in, but showing as a little black object against the hot western sky. Now he got his shoulder and knee up, and again he seemed to slip back until only his head was visible. Suddenly he vanished, and I could have fancied a faint shriek had reached me. I had a momentary impulse to go back and help him that my fears over-ruled.

90   Everything was then quite invisible, hidden by the deep pit and the heap of sand that the fall of the cylinder had made. Anyone coming along the road from Chobham or Woking would have been amazed at the sight – a dwindling multitude of perhaps a hundred people or more standing in a great irregular circle, in ditches, behind bushes, behind gates and hedges, saying little to one another, and that in short, excited shouts, and staring, staring hard at a few heaps of sand. The barrow of ginger-beer stood a queer derelict, black against the burning sky, and in the sand-pits was a row of deserted vehicles with their horses feeding out of nose-bags or pawing the ground.

from *The War of the Worlds* by H. G. Wells

* If alien creatures arrived on this planet, should we try to talk to them and learn from them or should we first try to demonstrate our own strength by attacking them? Or should we try to destroy them without trying to communicate at all?

1. Continue the story.

2. Below and on page 110 are some headlines which might appear in national newspapers after the discovery of the cylinder. Work out which headlines might appear:
    a. the day after the cylinder has been discovered,
    b. a week later,
    c. a month later.

Choose one of the headlines from each time and write the newspaper report that might have appeared beneath it.

TOP SECRET WEAPON TO BE USED ON ALIEN INVADERS?
MORE CYLINDERS DISCOVERED
FIRST CONTACT MADE WITH ALIEN CREATURES
TERROR FROM THE SKIES
SURRENDER LIKELY SOON
EXPERT CLAIMS: 'ALIENS MAY WANT PEACE'
SPACE INVADERS ATTACK
'STAY CALM' SAYS GOVERNMENT
NEW THREAT FROM MARS

FROM OUTER SPACE?
MARTIANS OFFER NEW TECHNOLOGY
ARMED FORCES BAFFLED BY ALIENS
'SURRENDER YOUR CITIES OR ELSE!' MARTIAN THREAT
MARTIAN ADVANCE HALTED

3. Write an account of what happened from the point of view of the shop assistant who was pushed into the crater by the crowd.

4. What might the Martians' first impressions of Earth have been? Write a translation of part of the Martians' log book, perhaps beginning with the journey from Mars.

5. Write the story of someone witnessing the arrival of some alien creatures on Earth. It could be part of a science fiction story, perhaps one of the opening chapters.

A Closer Look

1. What do the storyteller and most of the crowd expect to come out of the cylinder? Why are they horrified as well as shocked by what **does** appear?

2. The storyteller is repulsed and sickened by the sight of the Martians. What other emotions does he feel?

3. H. G. Wells describes the cylinder as the 'Thing'. What effect does the capital **T** on Thing have? (line 1)

4. Make a list of the words and phrases which make the reader strongly aware of the nastiness of what comes out of the cylinder. Here are two examples:
    'It glistened like wet leather.' (line 53)
    'A mouth . . . the lipless brim of which quivered and panted, and dropped saliva.' (lines 55 to 56)

5. Why does H. G. Wells include the phrase, **one might say**, in 'It was rounded, and had, one might say, a face.'? (line 54)

6. The book from which this extract is taken was published some time ago. Which of the following approximate dates for its publication do you think is most likely:
    1700
    1800
    1900
    1950?
Try to find good reasons for your choice and discuss your opinion with others.

Southbound on the Freeway

A tourist came in from Orbitville,
parked in the air, and said:

The creatures of this star
are made of metal and glass.

Through the transparent parts
you can see their guts.

Their feet are round and roll
on diagrams – or long

measuring tapes – dark
with white lines.

They have four eyes.
The two in the back are red.

Sometimes you can see a 5-eyed
one, with a red eye turning

on the top of his head.
He must be special –

the others respect him,
and go slow,

when he passes, winding
among them from behind.

They all hiss as they glide,
like inches, down the marked

tapes. Those soft shapes,
shadowy inside

the hard bodies – are they
their guts or their brains?

May Swenson

Looking at Advertisements

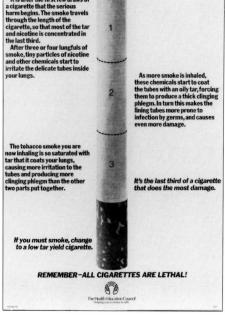

Advertisement no. 1   Advertisement no. 2

* What is the purpose of each of these advertisements?

* Is the purpose of each one the same?

* Which advertisement do you find more eye-catching? Why?

* What sort of person is each advertisement aimed at?

* Which advertisement conveys its message more quickly?

* Look at each advertisement separately and decide which of the following emotions or ideas the advertisement appeals to.

  a. logical thought and reason
  b. fear
  c. feelings of care for others
  d. common sense
  e. self-preservation
  f. guilt.

Does either advertisement appeal to any other ideas or emotions? Which appeal is most important in making the impact of each advertisement?

Advertisement no. 1
* How is the parent teaching the child to smoke?
* Would the appeal of the advertisement be different if either face in the picture were ugly?

Advertisement no. 2
* In order to get the message of this advertisement you have to spend a few minutes reading it. Does this mean that it is bound to be less effective than advertisement no. 1?

* Which of these advertisements would be more effective displayed in:

    a. a youth club
    b. a factory canteen
    c. a medical waiting room
    d. a school
    e. a railway or bus station
    f. a hoarding at the side of a main road?

Below are some more anti-smoking advertisements. Discuss each one using some of the questions above as a guide.

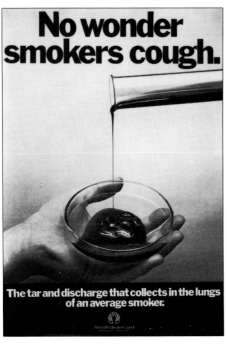

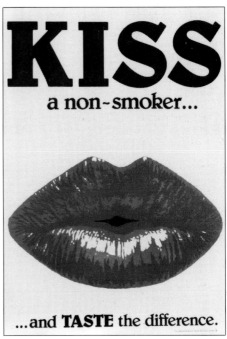

1. Choose several of these advertisements and write an essay comparing them, pointing out their appeal, their aims, their advantages and disadvantages, and their effectiveness.

I'VE GOT SOMETHING TO
TELL YOU

Breaking the News

Here is a short play in which a girl has to break some bad news to a teacher.
Read the play and then discuss the way the characters deal with the situation.

Carol :	Miss?
Teacher :	Yes, Carol?
Carol :	You know that thing at the end of term, with all the parents and that?
Teacher :	The Open Day. Yes?
Carol :	Well, I wanted to ask you. That is . . .
Teacher :	You're not getting nervous about that little play you're doing, are you, Carol? I've told you you'll be the star of the evening.
Carol :	No, I'm not nervous about it, Miss.
Teacher :	Well, what's the matter?
Carol :	My Mum and Dad have booked this trip, you see . . .
Teacher :	Yes?
Carol :	Well, we're going to see my uncle in Wales.
Teacher :	That's nice.
Carol :	No, you see, it's *then*.
Teacher :	What do you mean?
Carol :	I shan't be here. This trip, it's the last two days of term. (Pause)
Teacher :	You mean you're going to miss the Open Day?
Carol :	Yes, Miss.
Teacher :	Why didn't you tell me before?
Carol :	I've been meaning to, only . . .
Teacher :	How long have you known about this trip?
Carol :	Only a couple of days, Miss.
Teacher :	Well you could have said, Carol. It's a bit wet, I must say.
Carol :	I thought you'd be angry. I would have said earlier, but . . .
Teacher :	I was counting on you, you know. Do you have to go?
Carol :	I told my Mum. But she said it's the only time we can get away. My Dad works most weekends, you see.
Teacher :	Well, I'm very sorry, Carol. I suppose I'll have to try to find someone else.
Carol :	I *have* to go, Miss. I didn't want to. I mean, I want to see my uncle, but . . .
Teacher :	It's all right, Carol. I do understand.
Carol :	Will you get someone else to do it?
Teacher :	Well, I'll try. It's a bit short notice, really.
Carol :	Sorry.
Teacher :	Never mind, Carol. These things happen.

* Working with a partner, improvise scenes in which Carol and the teacher handle the situation quite differently. Here are some suggestions:

 Carol is very defensive, almost rude
 Carol is very casual
 Carol is very polite and concerned.
 Teacher is very calm
 Teacher becomes very angry
 Teacher is very formal and cold.

How does the way one character behaves affect the way the other one responds? Try to agree on the most successful approach for each character.

* Working with a partner, improvise the scenes described below. When you have worked on them you may choose to write and perhaps perform a script for one or more of them.

a. A teacher at school has lent you a book or a record. It has been damaged in an accident at home. You know that the book or record is difficult to replace because it is no longer available in shops. Break the news of what has happened.

b. You have been playing football in the garden with a friend, although your father has told you not to. Your friend kicks the ball into some dahlias which your father has been preparing throughout the summer for the local Show. Several flowers are badly damaged. Break the news to your father.

c. A few weeks ago you bought tickets for yourself and a friend for a rock concert. He paid you for his ticket but you are looking after it. You wait for him outside the hall on the night of the concert. He is so late that you think he must have been held up at work and is not coming. At last you sell his ticket to someone else. Just as you are about to go into the concert, your friend turns up. Break the news to him.

d. You and your best friend have both been trying for some time to get a place on a course or in a sports team. You have at last succeeded. You are very pleased and excited but also worried that your best friend will be jealous. Break the news of your success to him or her.

e. You have just discovered that you cannot go on holiday with a friend and his or her family because you have to visit relations with your older brother or sister. You are worried that your friend will think you have deliberately chosen not to go on the holiday. Break the news.

f. Your younger brother or sister has been pestering you for ages to take him or her with you when you go out with your friends. Finally you agree to do so. Break the news to your friends.

Waiting to Hear

Choose one of these beginnings and carry on the story.

1. Roger sat silently on one of the eight shabby seats in the corridor. Everything about him was quiet. There was a clean smell in the atmosphere: a mixture of furniture polish and disinfectant. He could see a thin shaft of sunlight slanting through the window.

   Far away in the distance he could just hear vehicles moving along on the motorway.

   He waited, trying hard not to panic, not to let his mind dwell on what had happened and what he should do now.

   A swing door at the end of the corridor opened and a middle-aged woman carrying a clip board under her arm, came towards him.

   'Mr Shaw?' she said.

2. Helen couldn't even drink her cup of coffee at breakfast, and, as for eating anything, well, that was quite out of the question.

   Her mother was usually a very patient person, but at last her nerves could stand no more.

   'Oh, do sit down and stop fidgeting, Helen. That won't make the postman come!' she said.

   'I'm sorry, but I can't help it,' said Helen. 'Do you think it'll come today?'

   'Well, how should I know, dear? I haven't got second sight.'

   'It's just that –'

   Helen broke off with a little snorting breath as the flap of the letter box on the front door clicked down.

   'I daren't go!' she said. 'I just daren't go.'

The Lesson

'Your father's gone,' my bald headmaster said.
His shiny dome and brown tobacco jar
Splintered at once in tears. It wasn't grief.
I cried for knowledge which was bitterer
Than any grief. For there and then I knew
That grief has uses — that a father dead
Could bind the bully's fist a week or two;
And then I cried for shame, then for relief.

I was a month past ten when I learnt this:
I still remember how the noise was stilled
In school-assembly when my grief came in.
Some goldfish in a bowl quietly sculled
Around their shining prison on its shelf.
They were indifferent. All the other eyes
Were turned towards me. Somewhere in myself
Pride, like a goldfish, flashed a sudden fin.

Edward Lucie-Smith

* What does the headmaster mean when he says, 'Your father's gone'?

* What is the boy's immediate reaction?

* What does the poet mean when he says, 'a father dead could bind the bully's fist a week or two'?

* What does the poet mean when he says, the 'goldfish . . . were indifferent'?

* What does the poet mean when he says, 'pride . . . flashed a sudden fin' in him?

* Why is the poem called 'The Lesson'?

* 'I cried for shame, then for relief.' Why does the boy feel ashamed and then relieved?

* The writer of the poem is an adult now; why do you think he chose this incident from his childhood as the subject for a poem?

* In the poem we learn about Edward Lucie-Smith's reactions to the news of his father's death. Basing your views on these reactions, and on hints we are given of his life in school, what sort of boy do you think he might have been?

Bad News

Andy and Sammy, his younger sister, are staying with some friends of the family, the Thompsons, who run a small hotel. Andy and Sammy are getting ready to go out to visit their mother, who is in hospital.

Andy had just finished, and was using the brush to give a last lick to his own hair, when suddenly he became puzzled by his realisation that Mrs Thompson was being uncommonly quiet on the phone, when all the time she usually shouted so loud you'd have thought she was trying to make herself heard without wires all the way clean to the city, over a hundred miles away. And it wouldn't surprise him if she *could* do it either; it wouldn't surprise him one bit. After all, he could hear her all the way up on the top of Dog's Head Rock when she called him, and his mother couldn't yell that loud. He doubted if even *Mr* Thompson could. But *Mrs* Thompson sure could; she just had to open that big mouth of hers and her voice went off like a siren. But now, now for the first time that he could remember, he couldn't hear her say a word. And it wasn't like Mrs Thompson to do all the listening.

Even Sammy noticed it. The two of them stood still, not moving at all, and hardly daring even to look at each other.

And then he heard Mrs Thompson say just three words: 'Oh my God!' so softly, almost inaudibly, that it didn't even sound like her. Then he heard the same words over again: 'Oh my God! How long ago did you say?'

But she didn't say any more. He heard the sound the phone always made when it was being replaced on its receiver, and the rooms of the hotel seemed even more silent than they did in the dead of night. There was always something wrong when Mrs Thompson stopped talking.

And then, even before he heard her slowly walking farther along to the bar, and after a while calling 'Bert! Bert!' in that same low, hoarse voice that was not at all like her real voice, and heard her whispering something to him, and Mr Thompson sounding shocked when he said something back, but both of them speaking too quietly for him to hear a single word – it was then he started to feel his own terrible fear. It made him turn cold all over; and yet, at the same time, terribly hot inside. His throat became cloyed with the taste he'd only known after being sick. He stood there, waiting, almost forgetting Sammy, who was just as still beside him. The whole room felt as though it was somehow straining towards him – the beds, the dresser with its long pocked mirror, the big bleak wardrobe, the picture of an old man smoking a pipe – they all seemed to be leaning over him, as though every brick of the hotel-building was about to fall in on them.

The door opened – so slowly that it was as though it was merely being pushed by the breeze, but as it opened, he could see Mrs Thompson was standing there. She still had her hat on, and the skirt of her costume, but not the coat.

But it was her face that he saw most of all. She looked suddenly years older. One weatherbeaten cheek kept twitching a little. Everything in her face looked as though it had suddenly sagged, even her eyes.

She was trying to say something, but each time she opened her mouth her cheek only twitched all the more. He felt as though he wanted to shout at her, she made him feel so impatient. He didn't know why; he just did. He wanted to yell out and tell her to say something. And yet, although he couldn't believe it, didn't want to *make* himself believe it, he knew what it was she was going to say.

'She's – she's dead, isn't she!'

He could hardly believe even these words were his own. The voice didn't sound like his, but like someone else's, a stranger's, the voice of a stranger who had come unheard and unseen into the room. Outside, he heard a dog bark. Even the men in the bar seemed to have stopped talking. Sammy was somewhere behind him. She must be standing perfectly still. Mrs Thompson still didn't move. The stillness of the room was like a long cold tautening of his nerves.

Mrs Thompson's face twitched again. Her mouth opened as though she was going to say something, but couldn't. All she could do was to make an ineffectual gesture with one of her large rough hands. He could see she was trying to make her face stop from suddenly crumpling up. The effort made the one cheek twitch all the more; and her eyes were suddenly moist.

'Andy,' she said at last, 'come into my room for a moment. You too, Sammy.' And she moved towards them.

But he knew what it was she was going to say. He knew his mother was dead. He knew that was what she was going to tell them. And he didn't want to hear it. He didn't want to hear anything. He *wouldn't* hear it yet. He wouldn't believe it – not until something inside him told him, finally, that it was true. He wasn't going to have someone else tell him, not even Mrs Thompson. He just wanted to get away, to get out of the cloying feeling of the room, and the whole building, and the touch of Mrs Thompson's large rough gentle hands.

'Come on, Andy. Come on, Sammy,' she was saying. But suddenly he couldn't stand it any longer. As she reached her hand towards him, he brushed past her, hearing her call 'Andy! Andy!' in shocked hoarse tones as, slamming the door behind him, he ran along the passage and out of the building.

from *A Waltz Through the Hills* by G. M. Glaskin

* What first makes the children suspect that something unusual is happening when Mrs Thompson is on the telephone?

* At what point in the story do **you** begin to suspect that something is wrong?

* Why does the writer at first point out how loud Mrs Thompson normally is, and then — after the news has arrived — keep reminding us of the silence?

* How can we tell that Sammy is aware that the news is bad?

* Andy has guessed that his mother had died and yet he will not allow Mrs Thompson to tell him the news. Can you understand why? Do you sympathise with him? What do you think you would do if someone was trying to tell **you** bad news which you had already guessed?

* Why does Andy run away?

* What would you do now if you were Mrs Thompson?

* What is the best way to break bad news — gradually or suddenly? Why? Does it depend on the person you are talking to and the circumstances?

1. Write about what happens in this scene from the point of view of Sammy or of Mrs Thompson.

2. Write a story about someone receiving or having to break bad news. It might be a complete story or just a chapter from a much longer one.

The Rumour

Shopping used to take all Saturday morning then. First we fetched coal
from the local depot, then we would race one another home, hoy the coal
into the cellar, and off again to the Co-op to queue for bread, or to Mrs
Ogle's for pies, or to one of Peter Pope's establishments for fruit and
vegetables. There were other fruit shops, of course, but they were for the
rich – foremen and others who went to work 'dressed' as we say. We made
do with Peter's more modest emporiums.

There were quite a number of these about town. They were
unobtrusive, 'The Pope', as the more ribald of our large Catholic
population always called him, didn't waste money on show. Any little
tumble-down shack, any derelict chip shop would do. He put a teenage girl
of uncertain scholarship in charge, provided her with a pair of scales and a
leather money wallet, dumped his crates of third-rate market stuff on the
unswept floor, and was ready for business.

We bought his wares in spite of these conditions because they were
cheap and most of our fathers were out of work. The Pope made quite a
profit, most of which he ate and drank. All day he went round his motley
collection of dumps checking up on the honesty and arithmetic of his Lilys
and Gladyses, and at one o'clock he would sit down to a gargantuan repast.
Fruit, vegetables, hot pease pudding, cold ham sandwiches, all were
shovelled in without discrimination and with an only too audible
enjoyment.

One Saturday these dietetic habits caught up with him and he died. Mrs
Gilhooly, hurrying to her local shack to get the pick of a poor lot of greens,
was told by a tearful little drudge who was just locking up. Naturally she
passed the news on. And when Mrs Gilhooly told Mrs Moran behind her
hand in the butcher's that the Pope was dead, she little thought what she
was starting. To tell Mrs Moran was to tell the parish and the news soon
spread up and down the tangle of streets between the river and the smoke-
blackened stone edifice dedicated to our local saint.

Presently a stream of people, mostly women, some carrying babies, many
wearing the first incongruous hat they had snatched up, were to be seen
streaming down the side streets that converged on the church. A high
sound of keening filled the air. When Father O'Hanrahan returned from a
hospital visit, he had to pick his way among ardent rosary sayers on the
very steps.

Inside the church a powerful volume of prayers was ascending. Every
bench was crowded. Beads rattled; pious ejaculations burst from full
hearts. For one wild moment he wondered if by some divine coincidence
the whole parish had simultaneously obeyed his oft-repeated injunction to
bring all their problems to Mother Church. Then, recognising a number

of extremely unlikely faces, he was forced to realise that this fervour at 10 a.m. on a Saturday morning had nothing to do with him.

Mrs Moran enlightened him in a hoarse whisper. 'It's his Holiness, Father. He's been called home. I had it from Mrs Gilhooly in the butcher's an hour ago.' Solemnly Father O'Hanrahan vested, and canalised the individual streams of prayer into a mighty upward fountain.

At one o'clock his housekeeper slipped in and whispered that the wireless news had not mentioned the Holy Father's demise – 'but you'd
50   expect that of the British, God save us.' She also told him that old Peter Pope the fruiterer was dead, and 'should she get her tatties and greens from the Co-op, Father?'

The awful truth began to dawn on Father O'Hanrahan. He turned the flow of prayer off like a tap and in a little while the church was empty. Housewife theologians, however, argued half the afternoon about their wasted prayers. What would happen to all those fervent petitions accidentally attributed to an event which, they tried to tell themselves, had happily not yet happened.

'Ah, sure,' said old Mrs Hegarty, 'They'll be saved up somewhere now
60   until His Holiness is taken.'

Many accepted this savings-bank view. Others thought their prayers might be transferable to other persons. Some frankly gave them up as lost. The debate was taken up by the men and carried on in the Rose and Shamrock until closing time. It almost ousted the inquest on the day's racing.

from *Two Lamps in our Street* by Arthur Barton

* Do you think that this could be a true story or is it too far-fetched to believe. Give reasons for your point of view.

* Who is chiefly responsible for passing on the rumour that the Pope has died?

1. What do you think Mrs Moran and Mrs Gilhooly might have to say to one another when they next meet? Write their conversation.

2. Write a story in which a piece of news is misunderstood, leading to much confusion.

3. Write a story with the title, *The Rumour.*

* How do rumours start?

* Is it possible to start a rumour about *any* subject?

* Which of these rumours would it be easiest to spread, do you think?
Why?

> The Isle of Wight has been submerged by a freak tidal wave.
> The school summer holiday this year is going to be one week
> shorter than usual.
> The failure of the tea crop in India is likely to increase the price of
> tea in Britain to over £1 for a small packet.

* In times of war people are advised not to listen to rumours. Why
should this advice be especially necessary in war time? How could an
enemy make use of rumour?

A Closer Look

1. Below on the left are two lists of words taken from *The Rumour*. The
first list is from the first four paragraphs of the story; the second list is
from the second part of the story. The meanings of the words are given
in the lists on the right, but these are not in the same order as the words
themselves. Choose the correct meaning for each word and test your
choice by looking back at the story.

emporiums (line 7)	abandoned
unobtrusive (line 9)	eating
ribald (line 9)	shops
derelict (line 11)	gigantic
motley (line 17)	discreet, inconspicuous
gargantuan (line 19)	building
audible (line 21)	assorted
dietetic (line 23)	coarse, rude
edifice (line 30)	noisy

incongruous (line 32)	at one and the same time
keening (line 34)	religious thinkers
ardent (line 35)	displaced, pushed aside
simultaneously (line 40)	unsuitable
injunction (line 40)	order
canalised (line 46)	mourning, wailing
demise (line 49)	prayers
theologians (line 55)	keen
fervent (line 56)	conducted
petitions (line 56)	heartfelt, enthusiastic
ousted (line 64)	death

2. Choose at least ten of the words from the left-hand lists and write a
very short story in which you use those words correctly.

Honoured Sir and Madam

Mr and Mrs Thornton's five children have sailed from Trinidad on their way to England. This is the letter which the captain of the ship, Captain Marpole, writes to Mr and Mrs Thornton from Havana, where the ship puts in to port unexpectedly.

Havana de Cuba

Honoured Sir and Madam,
I hasten to write to you to relieve you of any uncertainty!

After leaving the Caymans we stood for the Leeward Passage, and sighted the Isles of Pines and False Cape on the morning of the 19th and Cape S. Antonio in the evening, but were prevented from rounding the same by a true Norther, the first of the season, on the 22nd, however, the wind coming round sufficiently we rounded the cape in a lively fashion and stood NNE well away from the Coloradoes which are a dangerous reef lying off this part of the Cuban coast. At six o'clock on the morning of the 23rd there being light airs only I sighted three sail in the North-East, evidently merchantmen bound on the same course as ourselves, at the same time a schooner of similar character was observed standing out towards us from the direction of Black Key, and I pointed her out to my mate just before going below, having the wind of us he was within hailing distance by ten in the morning, judge then of our astonishment when he rudely opened ten or twelve disguised gun-ports and unmasked a whole broadside of artillery trained upon us, ordering us at the same time in the most peremptory manner to heave-to or he would sink us instanter. There was nothing to do but to comply although considering the friendly relations at present existing between the English and all other governments my mate was quite at a loss to account for his action, and imagined it due to a mistake which would be speedily explained, we were immediately boarded by about fifty or seventy ruffians of the worst Spanish type, armed with knives and cutlasses, who took possession of the ship and confined me in my cabin and my mate and crew forward while they ransacked the vessel committing every possible excess broaching rum-casks and breaking the necks off wine-bottles and soon a great number of them were lying about the deck in an intoxicated condition, their leader then informed me he was aware I had a considerable sum in specie on board and used *every possible threat which villainy could devise* to make me disclose its hiding-place, it was useless for me to assure him that beyond the fifty or so pounds that they had already discovered I carried none, he grew even more insistent in his demands, declaring that his information was certain, tearing down the panelling in my cabin in his search. He carried off my instruments, my clothes, and all

my personal possessions, even taking from me the poor Locket in which I was used to carry the portrait of my Wife, and no appeal to his sensibility, tho' I shed tears, would make him return this to him worthless object, he also tore down and carried away the cabin bell-pulls, which could be of no possible use to him and was an act of the most open *piracy*, at length, seeing I was obdurate, he threatened to blow up the ship *and all in it* if I would not yield, he prepared the train and would have proceeded to carry out this devilish threat if I had not in this last extremity, consented.

I now come to the latter part of my tale. The children had taken refuge in the deck-house and had been up to now free from harm, except for a cuff or two and the Degrading Sights they must have witnessed, but no sooner was the specie, some five thousand pounds in all mostly my private property and most of our cargo (chiefly rum sugar coffee and arrowroot) removed to the schooner than her captain, in sheer infamous wantonness, had them all brought out from their refuge your own little ones and the two Fernandez children who were also on board and murdered them, every one. That anything so wicked should look like a man I should not have believed, had I been told, tho' I have lived long and seen all kinds of men I think he is mad: indeed I am sure of it; and I take Oath that he shall be brought to at least that tithe of justice which is in Human hands, for two days we drifted about in a helpless condition, for our rigging had all been cut, and at last fell in with an American man-of-war, who gave us some assistance, and would have proceeded in pursuit of the miscreants himself had he not most explicit orders to elsewhere. I then put in to the port of Havana, where I informed the correspondent of Lloyds, the government, and the representative of the *Times* newspaper, and take the opportunity of writing you this melancholy letter before proceeding to England.

There is one point on which you will still feel some anxiety, considering the sex of some of the poor innocents, and on which I am glad to be able to set your minds at rest, the children were taken onto the other vessel in the evening and I am glad to say there done to death *immediately*, and their little bodies cast into the sea, as I saw with great relief with my own eyes. There was no time for what you might fear to have occurred, and this consolation I am glad to be able to give you.

I have the honour to be,
Your obedient servant,
JAS. MARPOLE,
Master, barque *Clarinda*

from *A High Wind in Jamaica* by Richard Hughes

In fact, Captain Marpole was mistaken — the children were not killed.

* If you were Mr and Mrs Thornton and you received this letter, how would you react?

* Captain Marpole begins his letter, '**I hasten to write to you to relieve you of any uncertainty.**' Does his letter live up to this promise?

* Do you find the letter: funny . . . shocking . . . upsetting . . . cold . . . inhuman . . . caring . . . foolish? Discuss your views with others in the class.

* What impression do you get of the character of Captain Marpole, the writer of the letter?

* What general advice would you offer Captain Marpole about the best way of writing a letter of this kind?

1. Make a list of the main items of news in the letter and put them in the order of their importance for Mr and Mrs Thornton.

2. Write the letter **you** would have written in Captain Marpole's place, before you knew that the children were still alive. You should include most of the news he gives, but you will probably want to change the order and you may decide to write in a more modern style.

3. Write the reply you would send to Captain Marpole if you were Mr or Mrs Thornton.

The New World

In 1492, when Christopher Columbus sailed west from Spain searching for a new land beyond the Atlantic Ocean, most people were convinced that the Earth was a flat disc and that if you sailed far enough, you would reach – and fall off – the rim of the world.

COLUMBUS (*writing in journal*).

> 'Friday, August the third, Fourteen-Ninety-Two: Set sail from the bar of Saltes in Palos at eight o'clock and proceeded with a strong breeze till sunset, fifteen leagues South afterwards South-West and South by West which is the direction of the Canaries.'

> 'September the sixth: Cleared from the Canaries and sailed due West.'

> 'September the ninth: Sailed this day nineteen leagues, and determined to count less than the true number, that the crew might not be discouraged if the voyage should prove long. . . .
> The sailors steered badly, causing the vessel to fall to leeward toward the North–East, for which the admiral reprimanded them repeatedly.'

From the captain's cabin you move back to the sailors.

BARTOLOMÉ.   Told us off he did. How can *us* help it?
FRANCISCO.   That's right. What do he think we are?
BARTOLOMÉ.   Damned galley slaves – that's what he thinks we are.
FRANCISCO.   Sooner be back in prison.
CARLOS.   You know what *I* think? I think he's mad.
FRANCISCO.   Reckon you're right. I'll tell 'ee what I saw only last night it was. I were on watch in the bits and there he were a-standing up on the forward castle, standing up there like a statue up on a church – and talking to himself he was, face didn't seem to move but he were a-talking to himself – talking right out loud to the sea and the moon.

Columbus is talking to himself.

COLUMBUS.   There are strange things happening.
DOUBT.   Beyond the horizon is nothing at all –
                 nothing at all.
COLUMBUS.   Nothing at all? That is not true,
           For the last few days there have been signs.

Floating grasses, a live crab –
Never found beyond eighty leagues of land;
A whale – whales are always near the land;
A floating branch with berries – that means land too.
And those white birds flying South-West –
Where could they be going if not to land?
Land . . . land . . . land . . .

FAITH.   Land is ahead, so be not depressed –

ECHO.   be not depressed.

DOUBT.   All is mirage. Disappointment is all –

ECHO.   disappointment is all.

FAITH.   Keep on your course. There is land in the West –
land in the West.

DOUBT.   Better turn back or worse will befall –
worse will befall.

COLUMBUS.   Better turn back? Turn back!
Who dares tell me that?
Man – or more than man – who dares use those words?

SPOKESMAN OF CREW.
Turn back, Captain, turn back.

COLUMBUS.   What's that? Who said that?

SPOKESMAN OF CREW.
'Turn back, Captain.' I said that.
I am the spokesman of your crew.
We have gone as long as we can.
We cannot go on any more.
We want to go back.
We want to go back.
We want to go back.

COLUMBUS.   Silence there!
So you want to go back?
You disappoint me, gentlemen.
Don't you know our voyage is nearly done?
We are within a few days' sail of land.

1ST VOICE.   Who says so?

COLUMBUS.   I say so, my friend. I have seen the signs.

2ND VOICE.   Signs!

Murmurs from the crew.

COLUMBUS.   All last night I heard – and so did you –
All last night we heard birds passing
Flying West-South-West.
That means land.

1ST VOICE.   I don't believe it.

2ND VOICE.   Why should it mean land?

COLUMBUS.   You fool! What else could it mean?

2ND VOICE.	I'll tell you what it could mean.
	Back in the seas of Europe birds are a sign of land
	But away out here on the rimless rim of the world
	Things are different, signs are no longer signs,
	And birds are no longer birds. How do we know
	These birds that pass in the night are not a trick.
	Of the Devil to lead us on
	To one mirage of land after another
	Until our food is gone and our ship falls to pieces
	And we ourselves are madmen, drowned in a mad sea?
1ST VOICE.	He's right, Captain, he's right.
	We've gone as far as we can. It's time to turn back.
CREW.	We want to go back.
	We want to go back.
	WE WANT TO GO BACK.
COLUMBUS.	Silence. You're wasting your time.
	I am Christopher Columbus. I do *not* turn back.
2ND VOICE.	Oh yes you will, if we say so.
1ST VOICE.	If you won't yield to reason, you'll yield to force.

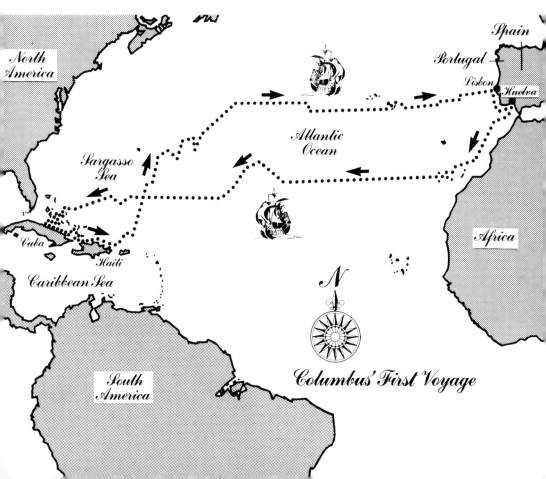

Columbus' First Voyage

SPOKESMAN OF CREW.
He's right, Captain. You can't keep on
If all your crew are against you.

COLUMBUS. I know that. Keep quiet.
Listen to me, Señores,
Today is October the eighth; it is my reckoning
We shall strike land within three days. Give me five –
If by then the land has failed us,
Then we shall reconsider what we must do.
Only wait five days. I know it in my heart
That land is over there. Señor Pinzón,
Captain of the *Pinta*, thinks so too –
And he, as you know, is a master seaman,
Well, Señores, if he and I are right,
All your troubles are over. What remains is glory –
Glory, my friends, and gold.
Gold, Señores, gold . . .
Give me five days more.

CREW (*to themselves*).
Gold . . . gold . . . gold . . . gold . . .

When their murmuring has faded away Columbus is heard
making another entry in his diary.

COLUMBUS. 'October the eleventh: This day the *Pinta* picked up a reed and a stick, and another stick carved, as it seemed, with iron tools . . . and some grass which grows on land . . . and a tablet of wood. The crew on seeing these signs breathed and felt great joy!'

BARTOLOMÉ. Hear what the *Pinta* found today?
FRANCISCO. Course I heard. Things be lookin' up.
BARTOLOMÉ. Captain's ordered a special watch. First as sights land, he'll get a rare reward.
FRANCISCO. What be time now?
BARTOLOMÉ. Near two hours till midnight. Dark night bain't it?
FRANCISCO. Ssh! Here comes Captain.
Pause.

COLUMBUS. All correct here?
BARTOLOMÉ. All correct, Captain.
COLUMBUS. Either of you seen anything?
BARTOLOMÉ.
FRANCISCO. } No, Captain, nothing.
COLUMBUS. Keep your eyes skinned.
What's that yonder?
BARTOLOMÉ. What, Captain?

FRANCISCO.	I can't see nothing.
COLUMBUS.	That little light.
FRANCISCO.	Light?
BARTOLOMÉ.	Light?
COLUMBUS.	You're blind, you fools, you're blind.
	Where's Pedro Gutiérrez? *He's* got eyes.
FRANCISCO.	I'll fetch him for 'ee, Captain.
COLUMBUS.	Light, of course it's a light . . . But it comes and goes,
	Like a taper of wax rising and falling –
BARTOLOMÉ.	Maybe it's just a star.
COLUMBUS.	Star, you fool?
	Who ever saw a star moving from side to side.
	Dipping and jerking? This –
	If it's not an illusion – this is a sign of life,
	This is a sign of land –
FRANCISCO.	Here 'ee be, Captain.
	Here's Gutiérrez, and Rodrigo Sánchez too –
	Another fellow with gimlet eyes.
COLUMBUS.	Come here, Gutiérrez. And you too, Sánchez.
	Look over there where I point.
	What do you see, Gutiérrez?
GUTIÉRREZ.	Where, Captain? I see nothing.
COLUMBUS.	Look where I'm pointing, damn you. Don't you see a light?
	No it's gone out now. Wait.
	Keep your eyes over there.
GUTIÉRREZ.	Right, Captain, I'm waiting.
COLUMBUS.	Now! Do you see it?
GUTIÉRREZ.	No.
COLUMBUS.	It's gone out again. Keep looking.
	Now!
GUTIÉRREZ.	Where? Where? . . . Mother of God!
	Yes, I see it.
	Yes, it *is* a light. A light.
COLUMBUS.	And you, Sánchez, do you see it?
SÁNCHEZ.	Can't say as I do.
COLUMBUS.	Don't you see any light?
SÁNCHEZ.	Nay, Captain. Can't see nothing.
COLUMBUS.	But you must. You must see it, you must.
SÁNCHEZ.	Nay, Captain, I don't.
COLUMBUS.	But you see it, don't you, Gutiérrez?
GUTIÉRREZ.	I see it surely. By God I see it.
COLUMBUS.	Then it is land at last.
FRANCISCO.	That's what *he* says.
BARTOLOMÉ.	Reckon he's right. It's land.

FRANCISCO.   Sánchez don't see it.
BARTOLOMÉ.   No, but Gutiérrez do.
FRANCISCO.   Well, we shall know at dawn.

Pause

CHORUS.   Look . . . Look . . . Look!
What do we see in the dawn?
Land . . . Land . . . Land!
Taking shape in the rising sun,
A green land with a golden beach,
A land of colour, a land of life,
A land, a land, a land!

from *Christopher Columbus* by Louis MacNeice

* What signs of fear and excitement do the members of the crew show in this extract?

* Why is Columbus so sure that land is near? Why don't the crew believe him?

* Sánchez does not see the light which Colombus and Gutiérrez see. How does this increase the tension of the scene?

* How can you tell that this extract is from a **radio** play?

1. It is several months later, when Columbus and his crew are back at home. Write down what Gutiérrez might tell his family about his first sight of land and what happened afterwards.

2. Columbus was travelling into completely unknown places, where anything might happen; today, almost the whole Earth has been explored, but there are still one or two areas of land and some deep ocean areas which are completely unknown to us. Imagine you are involved in an exploration of one of these areas. Write the story of how a remarkable new discovery is made.

3. A spacecraft is drifting at the furthest edge of space. All the data screens have gone blank. The commander is convinced that they are about to discover a new universe; the crew are not so sure. Write the story of what happens. You might choose to write it as a series of entries in the ship's log.

Starting a Play

Here is a conversation between two people, Adam and Jane, in which they discuss ideas for writing a play.

Adam: I've got this idea for a play. There's two kids messing about at the seaside. They're on a cliff. It's . . . it's Cornwall and there's some old mine workings around and one of the kids falls down an old mine shaft—

Jane: Is he killed?

Adam: No. Well, it's not really a mine *shaft*, just a sort of hole where the ground's fallen in because of the mine workings underneath.

Jane: Like a pot-hole.

Adam: Yeah. And the other one has to try and rescue him.

Jane: Is that all?

Adam: Well, it's all I've got so far.

Jane: What about their parents, their families?

Adam: I hadn't thought about that.

Jane: Maybe they're worried, because the kids are late . . .

Adam: Maybe they feel guilty because they let the kids play on their own.

Jane: Maybe there's a row . . .

Adam: About the kids?

Jane: Yes. But maybe they don't get on too well sometimes anyway. The parents, I mean.

Adam: Are they—I mean, is it just *one* family?

Jane: Maybe one of the kids is a friend.

Adam: Or not really a friend—maybe one of them pushes the other down the hole.

Jane: Yeah . . . No, that's no good, they wouldn't have been there together.

Adam: But maybe it's a kind of dare that goes wrong . . .

Jane: Yes, that's good!

Adam: And one lad dares the other one to go down this hole . . .

Jane: Who says they're both lads?

Adam: All right then: this lad dares this girl to go down the hole.

Jane: Why?

Adam: I . . . er . . . oh . . . well . . . I know! They've been playing with a ball or a frisbee or something, and it's gone down this hole . . .

Jane: Yeah. Could be.

Adam: O.K. Let's do it.

Jane: Maybe one of them just lost something down the hole . . . Anyway, what's going to happen in the end?

Adam: I dunno. Let's get it started and then see how it goes.

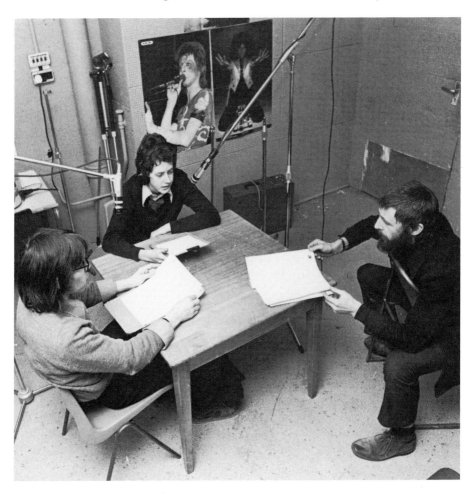

Jane: O.K. Hey, I've thought of something.

Adam: What?

Jane: We couldn't act all this out when it's written, anyway. Not
           someone trapped down a hole and someone else on top of
           the ground . . . And a scene at home.

Adam: That's O.K., we'll do it for radio . . . We'll tape it . . .

Jane: Yes, all right.

Adam: Where do we start?

Jane: Er . . . I know. The first scene is when the parents are sending
           the kids out because they want to talk about something . . .

1. Working with a partner, write the play which Jane and Adam might
have worked out. Note that they decided to write a **radio** play, to be
heard rather than seen. There is some advice about this kind of writing
on page 66 .

2. Working with a partner, plan and write a radio play. When you are
working, try to be open to as many ideas as possible and be prepared
to adapt your ideas to fit in with your partner's.

Colons in sentences

Sometimes the second part of a sentence explains or expands the first part. One way of showing this is to use the word **because** to link the two parts. For example:

> He enjoyed dancing because it helped him to relax.
> The car slid sideways without warning because one of the tyres had failed.
> People in Europe used to believe that it was dangerous to sail a long way to the west because they thought the ship would fall off the edge of the Earth.

Another way of showing the link between the two parts of the sentence is to use a colon : instead of the word **because.**

> He enjoyed dancing : it helped him to relax.
> The car slid sideways without warning : one of the tyres had failed.
> People in Europe used to believe that it was dangerous to sail a long way to the west : they thought the ship would fall off the edge of the Earth.

Read the sentences below and decide which ones **could** be linked by colons and which ones should remain separated by full stops. Usually a colon is suitable if you can link the sentences with the word because.

1. It's difficult to talk to anyone properly in Rachel's house. The television is always blaring.

2. I no longer wanted to compete in any of the track or field events. All my enthusiasm had gone.

3. From on the stage there came a loud shout, followed by an urgent sigh and then a dull thud. Someone had left the trap door open.

4. 'This is the nine o'clock news. Nothing of any interest has happened anywhere today as far as we know.'

5. Rasputin the parrot had a rich but limited vocabulary. He had spent eighteen years of his life on a merchant ship.

6. There was no doubt why Lee was quickly promoted to the first team. His father was one of the club's directors.

7. The man walked out of the shop. It was raining.

8. Robbie refused to wear the shirt. He thought it made him look soft.

9. I hate medical examinations. They are so embarrassing.

10. The post card was colourful and picturesque. It had taken three weeks to arrive from Majorca.

11. Our holiday in Ibiza was not a success. Grandma was ill for a week with flu and the sun refused to shine.

12. The ship gave a sickening lurch. It had struck a rock.

13. Motor racing can be a dangerous sport. There are many hazards and the pace is fast.

14. Tastes in public entertainment change across the years. Television has almost replaced films these days.

15. The weather forecast for tomorrow is miserable. It's going to rain for most of the day and it's going to be cold.

16. Our evening newspaper is always wet and torn. Rover always insists on bringing it home in his mouth.

17. The supermarket manager had to introduce many new lines in order to stay in business. A rival store had been opened in the town.

18. Finally the bus arrived. There was not even room to stand.

19. Adèle hated having to lie in bed all day. When she was fit she was a very active person.

20. Angela braked hard, almost falling over the handlebars. A broken bottle lay on the road in front of her.

Semi-colons in sentences ;

Usually we separate one sentence from the next with a full stop.
For example:

> The boy stood very still. Behind him the street was empty.

> The barricade was right across the road. The girl at the wheel of the car braked, swerved and then seemed to turn the car around, still at speed, in one easy, swinging movement.

Sometimes there is an unusually strong **link** between the subject matter of two sentences. For example:

> Alison is a very quiet person. She almost never raises her voice.

> 'I'm afraid I lost my temper. He shouldn't have teased me.'

In cases like this, we can show that **link** by using a slightly weaker stop than the full stop. We can use a semi-colon:

> Alison is a very quiet person; she almost never raises her voice.

> 'I'm afraid I lost my temper; he shouldn't have teased me.'

Sometimes two sentences have an unusually strong **link** because they balance one another. For example:

> I like fish and chips. My friend hates them.

> I like to stay in bed in the morning as long as possible.

> My dad always gets up early.

Here again we can show this strong link between two balanced sentences by using a semi-colon:

> I like fish and chips; my friend hates them.

> I like to stay in bed in the morning as long as possible; my dad

> always gets up early.

Here are twenty pairs of sentences; each pair is separated by a full stop. Decide which ones **could** be linked by semi-colons.

> 1. The second world war finished long ago. The stories about it continue.

> 2. Shelley was determined to slim. She ate nothing but bran and high-fibre foods.

> 3. My new camera cost me £75. The pictures are no better than those I got using my old camera.

4. Mrs Simms works at the supermarket check-out. Someone once gave her a gold sovereign instead of a 5p piece.

5. Some of the windows in the Youth Centre had been broken. Nobody could find out who had done it.

6. The motorway was blocked by an accident. We were forced to drive on the hard shoulder.

7. Some say computers will solve all our problems. Others say they are becoming our masters.

8. I almost fainted. It was the shock, I suppose.

9. One of my two uncles works in a car factory. The other one has been unemployed for three months.

10. Govind opened the door. He turned on the light and looked around.

11. The first strike lasted just over two weeks. The second one was much longer.

12. The water looked very inviting. Tracy wondered if she dared swim in it.

13. As a player he was mediocre. As a manager he was magnificent.

14. The whining overhead was louder now. The crowd was getting restless, looking up and around, trying to see where the noise was coming from.

15. The music surged and plunged, and then roared to new heights. It was overpowering.

16. 'Never mind what it looks like. Think how comfortable it will be.'

17. Melanie was a solitary girl. She sat lonely in her desk all day, refusing anyone's attempts at friendship.

18. This idea, then, was going to be just like all the rest. She was bitterly disappointed.

19. Leo revved his bike outside the staff room window. Like puppets on a single string, the teachers rose to their feet and glared out.

20. Crossing the river was easy. It was the next part that would cause the problems.

Making Words

Many words can be joined together to make new words:

card and board make cardboard
rail and way make railway
head and strong make headstrong.

Some joined words use older English words which we rarely use on their own any more, so they are not so obvious:

wright is an old English word for a maker of things, so:
a playwright is a maker of plays
a wheelright is a maker of wheels.

Some joined words are made from words or part-words from Latin and Greek. These words are not always obviously joined words at all, but they can be puzzled out. Try these examples:

1. Supernatural means above or beyond nature;
   sonic means travelling at the speed of sound;
   what does supersonic mean?

2. A biologist is someone who studies the science of living things;
   geology is the study of the science of rocks;
   what is a geologist?

3. A monograph is a piece of writing on one particular subject;
   a monoplane is an aeroplane with one set of wings;
   a television is a device for viewing objects or events at a distance;
   what is the device called a telegraph used for?

4. Insular means cut off, or surrounded by water;
   a peninsula is a piece of land which is almost surrounded by water;
   ultimate means last;
   what does penultimate mean?

5. Ante meridian (a.m.) means before noon;
   post meridian (p.m.) means after noon;
   natal (like nativity) means connected with birth;
   what is an ante-natal clinic?
   What is post-natal care?

6. Transatlantic means across the Atlantic Ocean;
   if you transplant something, you uproot it and re-plant it in another place;
   something that is portable can be carried about;
   what do you do if you transport something?

7. A **telemeter** is a device for measuring things at a distance;
   a **micrometer** is a device for measuring very small lengths or
   angles;
   a **telescope** is a device for looking at objects at a distance;
   what is a **microscope**?

8. A **subway** is a path or way under a road or building;
   terrain (like territory) means ground;
   what does **subterranean** mean?

9. **Medium** means middle;
   how does the **Mediterranean** Sea get its name?

10. **Primary** means first;
    primeval (sometimes **primaeval**) means belonging to the first
    stage of history;
    what does **medieval** (sometimes **mediaeval**) mean?

11. **International** means between nations;
    to **rupture** something is to break or burst it;
    what do you do if you **interrupt** something (such as a
    conversation or an electrical current)?

12. **Antifreeze** protects against freezing;
    anti-government means against the government;
    a **cyclone** is a wind system in which the winds move inwards
    towards its centre; what is an **anti-cyclone**?

13. To **co-operate** means to work together;
    to **co-educate** means to educate boys and girls together;
    what does to **co-exist** mean?

14. A **polygon** is a figure with many sides;
    a **monogamist** is a person who has one spouse;
    a **bigamist** is a person who has two spouses;
    what is a **polygamist**?

15. A **biography** is the story of someone's life;
    an **automobile** is a thing which moves itself, under its own
    power;
    an **automaton** (like automatic) is a machine which operates
    itself;
    what is an **autobiography**?

16. To **dictate** something is to say it (usually for someone else to
    write it down);
    to **predict** something is to say it will happen before it does;
    something that is **contrary** is against or the opposite of
    something else;
    what do you do if you **contradict** someone?

17. A **suicide** is someone who kills himself;
insecticide is a substance used to kill insects;
a **herb** is a plant;
what is **herbicide**?

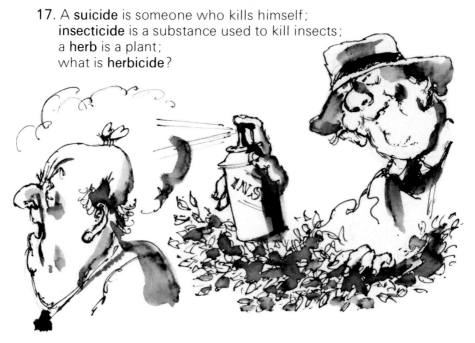

18. To **benefit** someone is to do good to them;
a **benefactor** is someone who does good to someone else;
when something **malfunctions** it works badly;
when someone is **malevolent** he wishes bad things towards other people;
what is a **malefactor**?
What does **benevolent** mean?

Look back at the puzzles you have just done and see if you can now work out the meanings of the following, which are called **prefixes** because they are attached to the beginnings of words:

super-	auto-
sub-	tele-
mono-	trans-
bi-	inter-
poly-	co-
pre-	pen-
ante-	micro-
post-	bene-
prim-	male-
medi-	contra-
anti-	

Beginnings

The beginning of a piece of writing often sets the atmosphere or 'tone' of what follows. Read the five beginnings below.

> One is the beginning of a true story;
> one is the beginning of a book about a scientific subject;
> one is the beginning of a story for young children;
> one is the beginning of an autobiography;
> one is the beginning of a thriller.

* Which is which?

* How can you tell? How many clues can you find in the way each one is written?

1. Winter came early to the city that year. Josiah Davidson, emerging from the subway, his arms loaded with schoolbooks, shivered against the dank November rain which blew icily against his face and sent a trickle down the back of his neck. He did not see three boys in black jackets who moved out of a sheltering doorway and stalked him.

Uncomfortable, unaware, he hurried along the street until he came to a run-down tenement. Here he let himself in through the rusty iron gate that led to the basement apartment.

The three boys went silently up the brownstone steps and took cover in the doorway, listening, waiting.

2. As a matter of historical fact I know that I was born in 1903 when we were living in Douglas Street, Cork, over a small sweet-and-tobacco shop kept by a middle-aged lady called Wall, but my memories have nothing to do with living in Douglas Street. My memories begin in Blarney Street, which we called Blarney Lane because it follows the track of an old lane from Cork to Blarney. It begins at the foot of Shandon Street, near the river-bank, in sordidness, and ascends the hill to something like squalor. No. 251, where we lived, is one of the cottages on the right near the top, though I realise now that it would be more properly described as a cabin, for it contained nothing but a tiny kitchen and a tiny bedroom with a loft above it. For this we paid two and sixpence — sixty cents — a week.

3. There were no oceans 4600 million years ago, when the Earth took shape, most likely from a vast shrinking cloud of dust. Crushed and heated by the shrinking process, its solids would have largely changed to molten rock. The lightest elements rose towards the surface. Some escaped as gases. Others formed a

seething sea of liquid rock. In time, surface rocks cooled and hardened into rafts that coalesced to build a solid crust. Meanwhile, volcanoes spewed steam and other gases into the hot, prehistoric atmosphere.

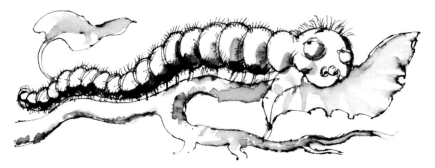

4. One day a small green caterpillar was quietly munching a large green leaf. The caterpillar had a large appetite for leaves and when he had finished chewing up the best bits of one leaf, he moved on to the next. Leaves were his favourite food. Soon the caterpillar had left a pattern on leaf after leaf as he munched his way up the tree. On his journey along the branch the caterpillar met a chockchafer.

'How lucky you are to have wings,' he said. 'I wish I could fly like everyone else round here.'

5. At 10.30 on a warm evening in 1902, Captain Peattie, master of the sailing ship *Leicester Castle*, was lying on his bunk, composing himself for sleep. He was a tough but amiable man from Paisley in Scotland, and he liked to read a page or two before turning out his lamp. It helped him relax.

The *Leicester Castle* was ghosting through the calm waters of the Pacific at a speed of three and a half knots. About 300 miles away to the south lay the Pitcairn Islands, where the *Bounty's* mutineers had settled. But, at this moment, Captain Peattie's thoughts were far removed from the *Bounty*, or mutiny, or any of the hazards which, from time to time, have threatened the safety of men at sea.

The book was a good one and, in any case, Captain Peattie had nothing to cause him any anxiety. Since they had sailed from San Francisco on passage to London, the going had been good. Right now, he wished there were more wind, but he had to admit that the calm, warm weather was very agreeable.

1. Try writing some beginnings of your own and see if others in the class can tell what sort of book you might have been beginning.

2. Here are some more beginnings. Choose one of them or one of your own beginnings and write a second paragraph, keeping the same tone and pace as the first one. You might try to carry on one piece of writing for a whole chapter or more, perhaps working with a partner writing alternate paragraphs.

1. Even as a young child, I knew that my parents had wanted a boy when I was born. This fact hasn't had as much influence on my life as you might expect, but it has helped to make me very conscious of being a girl and of having to prove myself in almost everything I do. I remember very clearly many of the 'firsts' of childhood: the first time I went to school, my first fight with another child, my first really serious illness.

2. Predicting, or forecasting, the weather has been an important part of people's lives for a very long time. Farmers and fishermen have an interest in the weather for obvious reasons; and in areas liable to long periods of drought or storm, 'experts' have often been called upon to predict or even influence the weather.

3. The air was so still and hot, it seemed to press down on the wooden houses and the dusty street. The calm was oppressive, like a giant cushion suffocating the town. There was no movement. Even the butcher's old hound lay perfectly still in the shadow of the shop doorway. Into this stillness came a single sound – the plaintive whistle of a locomotive. The townspeople heard the sound and they were afraid.

4. The sun shone. The birds sang. It was a perfect September morning. The mouse in the corner of the cornfield was happy. He lifted his nose and sniffed the breeze. He could smell no danger, so he set off across the field to see his friends, the moles, who lived under the pasture beyond the hawthorn hedge.

5. At dawn on the 26 October 1953, the lifeboat *Ambrose* plunged into the waves of Grantley Bay and began to work its way out to sea, heading east. It lumbered across the swell, its engines labouring so that the deck shook and shivered in sympathy. At the summit of each wave it tottered for a moment and then wallowed on into the trough beyond. The coxwain looked at his watch: six o'clock. There was only an hour before the high tide which must surely break the back of the *S.S. Primrose*. He considered the chances of rescuing her crew and decided he did not like the odds. He edged the throttles a little wider open and tightened his grip on the wheel.

RUNWAY ONE

AIRPORT RUNWAY TO BE EXTENDED?
Arguments begin again at Thornley

Local opposition to the proposed extension of the main runway at Thornley Airport has increased since last week. Then, the local Council disclosed its plans to interest a group of airline companies and travel firms in a revised scheme to extend the runway from 1646 metres to 2332 metres.

Plans to extend the runway were first put forward in 1979. These were dropped after a lengthy inquiry and after strong protests from local residents, teachers' representatives and conservationists. The protesters argued then that the runway's extension would allow heavier planes carrying more passengers to land, thus creating more noise and pollution, and congestion on the already over-crowded roads would increase. A spokesman for the protesters at the time said, 'An extended runway would bring no direct benefit to the people living in the area.'

These views were upheld by the chairman of the inquiry, despite the arguments of those in favour of the extension. These included the local Chamber of Commerce and the Department of Employment. They predicted increased prosperity within Thornley District Area as a direct result of the airport's expansion. They rejected claims that a longer runway would bring more pollution: 'People do not seem to realise,' said Mrs Jane Anstruther, then chairwoman of the Airport Development Committee, 'that a longer runway means larger aircraft and more people, and hence more jobs. And, because these planes are capable of carrying more passengers, the number of flights each day will actually go down.'

In the end, it was not the inquiry but a shortage of money which prevented the proposed runway extension from going ahead. The economic recession at the time meant that the Thornley extension plan was shelved. Now the fight is on again.

THORNLEY AIRPORT:
FACTS AND FORECASTS

	Length of main runway	Average no. flights per year	Average no. passengers carried per year	Average no. tonnes of freight lifted per year
1960s	1200m	6,000	180,000	150
1970s	1646m* (*from 1971)	8,000	300,000	335
1980s to 1990s	2332m* (*if further extended)	7,000	450,000	900

Transcript of an interview between *Sunday Post* reporter Chris Wallis and Mrs Anne Warren of 15, Allenby Avenue, Thornley.

Wallis	Mrs Warren, you live on the Foxton estate. Are you affected at the moment by aircraft using Thornley Airport?

Include in the introduction to the article

Mrs Warren: Yes, I am. The main thing is the noise.

Wallis: And will the problem of noise be increased for you if Runway One is extended?

Mrs Warren: It's bound to, isn't it? I mean, the planes will be lower. And if they've only just taken off, they'll be climbing really steeply. It'll be terrible.

Wallis: How often do planes pass over the estate at present?

Mrs Warren: Oh, about one every thirty or forty minutes or so, I suppose. About that.

Intro-duction

Wallis: And during the night?

Mrs Warren: Not so many, but in a way it's worse then. Especially if the odd one comes over lower than usual - it gives you a bit of a shock.

Wallis: And if the planes were lower all the time?

Mrs Warren: It'd be impossible. It's bad enough now. You can hardly hear the television some nights for the noise they make.

Wallis: Do you have double-glazing? I understand there are grants for that.

Mrs Warren: Yes, we do, but you can't double-glaze the garden, can you? And I like to have the windows open a bit sometimes.

Wallis: You have two children, I believe, Mrs Warren?

Mrs Warren: Yes, that's right.

Wallis: How old are they?

Mrs Warren: Sandra's fourteen and Simon's twelve.

Wallis: Do they go to the local school?

Mrs Warren: Yes, they both go to Foxton Park Comprehensive.

Wallis: And is the school close to the flight path?

Intro-duction

Mrs Warren: Yes, it's terrible some days. It seems to depend on the wind direction. So they say. Some days they seem to come right in on top of the school.

Wallis: Do your children complain?

Mrs Warren: They're used to it. But it must be affecting their studies and that. I work at the school at dinner times - I'm in the canteen, you know, supervising the kids. Some days it's awful. The noise.

Wallis: Would it make a lot of difference, though, if the runway was extended?

Mrs Warren: Of course it would. The planes will be bigger, won't they, so they'll make more noise. And they'll be lower. And what if - God forbid - what if there was an accident? What if a plane came down on the houses or on the school? What then? It could happen, whatever they say. Then there'd be questions.

Wallis: Some experts say that a longer runway would give a greater margin of safety, even with the bigger planes.

Mrs Warren: Well let the 'experts' come and live here then, and send their kids to school here. That's all I can say. It's all very well talking about safety when you don't have to live with the worry every day. And they don't have to put up with the noise either.

Having written up his interview, the reporter has picked out some of the things that Mrs Warren said and underlined them because they would be suitable quotations to use in the final article which is printed on page 154. The reporter has also made notes on some other parts of the interview. In the final article for the newspaper much of what Mrs Warren said will be summarised by the reporter.

The reporter also interviewed some other people in Thornley in order to get material for more articles. One of the people Chris Wallis interviewed was James Swinhoe, local businessman and chairman of Thornley Chamber of Trade. The article which Chris Wallis wrote for his newspaper as a result of that interview is printed on page 154.

Every day about twenty-five aircraft land or take off at Thornley Airport. Most of these aircraft use the main Runway One. If the proposed extension of the runway goes ahead, bigger and heavier aircraft will pass over nearby Foxton housing estate at a lower altitude.

Mrs Anne Warren, a resident of the threatened estate said that her main worry is that the noise level on the estate would be drastically increased if the runway were extended. 'It'd be impossible,' she said. 'It's bad enough now. You can hardly hear the television some nights for the noise.' Mrs Warren's house has been double-glazed using money from government grants, but as she pointed out: 'You can't double-glaze the garden.'

Mrs Warren's two children attend the comprehensive school on the estate and she works there as a school meals supervisor. Mrs Warren complained bitterly about the aircraft noise at the school: 'It's terrible. Some days they seem to come right in on top of the school.' She feels that the children's studies at the school are already being affected by the noise which, she claims, will get worse if the runway is extended: 'The planes will be bigger, so they'll make more noise,' she argues.

Safety is another major cause for concern at Thornley. As Mrs Warren put it, 'What if a plane came down on the houses or the school?' And Mrs Warren has a ready reply for those 'experts' who claim that the extension of the runway would improve safety. 'Let them come and live here and send their children to school here. It's all very well talking about safety when you don't have to live with the worry every day.'

Mr James Swinhoe, owner of a building firm in Thornley employing about fifteen men, is President of the Rotary, and Chairman of the Chamber of Trade. He was interviewed in the smart restaurant of Thornley Airport Terminal. As a BAC 111 arrived from Heathrow, he said, 'That's a service that's becoming increasingly popular with local business men and holiday makers. People have discovered how quick and easy it is to fly to and from here to Heathrow, without all the inconvenience of railways and the hassle of driving up the motorway. The journey only takes about an hour, so you can be in London for 10.30 and back again in the office before teatime.'

When asked why the local Chamber of Commerce were so keen that the extra traffic should come here to Thornley, Mr Swinhoe said, 'The advantages are considerable. We're very centrally located. You can get to most of the principal nothern cities from here. It would bring extra business to the town: a hotel; more offices for the airlines; above all, more employment for local people, especially the youngsters. And it would be permanent, not just seasonal employment. Some casual jobs would be provided as well, during the summer months, because of the increased number of tourists travelling on package holidays and charter flights.'

Many local people are opposed to the runway extension but that doesn't worry Mr Swinhoe. He said, 'It's swings and roundabouts. We've got to move with the times. Some people may suffer slightly more disturbance but at least—if we get this runway extended—their children should have jobs. If we don't get it, heaven help them.'

As he spoke the announcer's voice on the loudspeaker called passengers for one of the twice-weekly flights to Amsterdam. Perhaps in ten years' time Mr Swinhoe's dream will be fulfilled, and passengers will be taking off from Thornley for Bangkok, Los Angeles and Montreal.

* How would the proposed runway extension affect the following:

noise levels on the Foxton housing estate;
the number of aircraft landing and taking off at Thornley Airport each day;
the work of pupils and teachers at Foxton Park Comprehensive School and other schools in the area near the airport;
the number of permanent jobs available in Thornley;
the number of cars and buses travelling through Thornley;
the number of lorries on the roads in and around the town;
the general prosperity of the place?

The reporter talked with other Thornley people who had strong views about the proposed runway extension. Here are some of them:

Angela Ogilvy,
youth employment
officer

Arthur Campbell,
airline representative

Erik Casper,
unemployed
teenager

Doctor Kishore Sharma,
head of the accident unit
at Thornley hospital

Mrs Rachel Gardiner,
headmistress of Foxton
Park Infants School

Sandra Owen, pupil at
Foxton Park Comprehensive School

Jane Cooper,
unemployed teenager,
qualified secretary

Peter Lowe, package tour
operator

John Alerton,
teacher at Foxton
Park Comprehensive School

Judith Kears, owner/manager
of a small local hotel

* Which of the people pictured on pages 155 and 156 would you expect to support the proposed runway extension? Why?

* Which of the people pictured on pages 155 and 156 would you expect to oppose the runway extension? Why?

1. Look at the transcript of Chris Wallis's interview with Mrs Warren and the article that was based on it on pages 152, 153 and 154.
   Working with a partner improvise the interviews the reporter might have with some of the people pictured on pages 155 and 156.
   The reporter should make notes on some of what is said in the interview or – if this is possible – he or she could record the interview on tape and then transcribe it (that is, write it down from listening to the tape).

2. Working from the notes or transcripts of two interviews write the reporter's articles based on those conversations. One article should try to bring out the arguments in favour of the proposals; the second article should emphasise the arguments against the proposals.

3. There is to be an inquiry, led by Mrs Anne Elton Q.C., at which everyone's views on the proposed Runway One extension will be considered. Imagine you are one of the people who will be most affected by the plans and present your views to the inquiry in the form of a letter to Mrs Elton.

4. A public meeting is to be held in Thornley Town Hall so that local people can air their views about the proposed Runway One extension. Choose someone to act as chairperson at the meeting. Imagine you are someone who lives or works in the town. Your life or work would be affected by the proposed changes at the airport. You decide to make a speech at the meeting to say what you think. Working in rôle, make notes to support your point of view and then make your speech. The chairperson should be in charge of the meeting and should ask people to speak in turn.
   When several people have made their speeches the chairperson should open up the discussion so that other people in the meeting can give their views or reply to points made in the speeches. After all the opinions have been heard, a vote could be taken to find out how many people are in favour of the plans and how many people are against them.

Did You Ever Hear About . . . ?

. . . Talking about that sort of thing, did you ever hear what happened to me wife's sister? It was last autumn, October I think. No, I tell a lie — when we had all that rain: November, that was it.

Anyway, she'd driven over to see her mother in Allertondale, had Vera. She's getting on you know (her mother, I mean, not Vera) and now that she's on her own since the old man died, Vera goes over in her Mini about once a month.

This time she got a bit delayed starting back, it seems. Her mother had had a fall, putting out the milk bottle two days before. Do you know she was lying there for half an hour before her neighbour found her, poor old soul? So Vera didn't set off back home until it was just getting dark, and it was raining stair rods all the way across the moors to Bannen Cross. She said you couldn't see more than a few yards in front of you and she's not too fond of driving at the best of times, isn't Vera.

She'd just got past Bannen Cross when it eased up a bit, but it was still raining enough to wet you through, and she'd just passed the last house out of the village when she saw this woman at the bus stop on Enderby Road. Well, Vera knew from experience there wouldn't be another bus for at least two hours, and there was this woman almost drenched to the skin.

She was just wondering if she ought to give her a lift (and you know, Vera's not a silly person) when the girl half put out her hand as though she wanted Vera to stop but daren't thumb a lift properly. Anyway, to cut a long story short, Vera pulled up and gave the woman a lift. She said she seemed a very respectable woman; she had a nice woollen suit on, and a head-scarf, but no coat. Just a handbag with her.

They got talking, of course. It seemed the girl had been visiting her sister at Bannen Cross. She'd got off the bus and then found that her sister was away for the day and not expected back till midnight at the earliest. So she was stuck: all she could do was wait for the bus back again — there's nothing at all in Bannen Cross, it's only a few houses and a shop. Not even a pub to wait in. So she'd stood at the bus stop and then the rain had started. Vera said she was really grateful for the lift.

She said they got on really well together, talking about this and that, and then, well . . . They were just going up that very steep bit near Enderby Top when a map slid off the shelf in front of the girl onto her feet, so she put her hand to the floor to pick it up.

And then Vera noticed: on the back of the girl's wrist there was a lot of black hair — she hadn't seen it before because of the suit covering it—far too much for a woman to have. And Vera realised: she was in the middle of a dark moor, alone in the car with a man dressed as a woman!

Well, she's a sensible person, as I said, is Vera. She doesn't panic easily. She didn't scream or do anything foolish, she just thought: how do I get rid of him?

Then she had an idea. They were doing about sixty-five going down that long slope from the Top, and she thought, right, now for it. She pushed her foot down on the accelerator hard; then took her foot off it; then jammed on the brake, and the car stalled. The 'girl' was flung about a bit and Vera said, 'My God, what's up? What's up with this car?' And the 'girl' said, 'What's the matter?' And Vera said, 'I don't know, it did this yesterday *and* last week.'

The 'girl' said, 'Well, what do we do?' And Vera said, 'Well, yesterday, I got out and gave it a push, and last week Jack did it. Would you mind, dear, it shouldn't be too hard, we are on a hill.'

So the 'girl' said she would, and you don't need me to tell you what

Vera did then: as soon as 'she' — he — was behind the car, Vera was off like a bat out of hell. She went about a mile before she even stopped to close the passenger door properly.

And that's not quite the end of the story, either. While she was closing the door, reaching over the passenger seat, she saw the handbag that the man had been carrying, fallen on the floor of the car.

And then (she told my wife later on) she thought, with seeing this handbag lying there, well, perhaps I'm being a wee bit silly. Maybe I'm imagining things; maybe he was just a bloke who was going to a fancy dress party, or just liked dressing up. It didn't mean to say he was going to hurt anybody.

She did think about turning round to pick him up again, but then she thought better of it and started for home. Then, as she was getting into the town just where that bit of dual carriageway is, she realised she was quite near to the police station, so she thought, well, I may as well go and tell them, and hand in this bag. You never know, it might be helpful.

So she drove to the police station and they listened to her story. Vera said they were very nice to her but you could tell they weren't really taking it seriously. Anyway, they took down her statement and then the sergeant said they'd best just look in the bag to see if there was any clue to the man's identity in it, although that he doubted.

So they opened the handbag. And do you know what was in it?

An axe, with blood on the blade!

* Do you believe this story?

* Have you ever heard this story before, or one like it?

* Do you know any other stories about people having lucky escapes from danger, or stories about remarkable coincidences?

* How can you tell that this story is usually told, not read?

* Why does the storyteller include details such as the old lady falling when putting out the milk bottles, and the fact that the police station is near a section of dual carriageway?
Would it make any difference to the effect of the story if details like this were left out?

* Why do you think people often enjoy hearing stories like this, even if they are not really sure that they believe them?

1. Write a story of this kind — it could be one which has been told to you at some time — and try to make it sound as though someone is **telling** it.

Tall stories, especially those told by travellers, are not new. Here is one from the eighteenth century:

. . . It was during the recent siege of Gibraltar that I went with a supply fleet under Lord Rodney's command to see my old friend General Elliot, who, you will no doubt remember, has been much praised and decorated for his work in defending Gibraltar. General Elliot was overjoyed to see me, and after he had greeted me very warmly, we went to inspect the state of the garrison and take a look at what the enemy was doing.

Now, I had brought with me from London an excellent refracting telescope which I had bought at Dollond's, a most reputable firm. With the aid of this telescope I observed that the enemy were going to fire a thirty-six pounder cannon at the exact spot where we were standing. I told the general what was happening and he, using the telescope, saw that I was right. Immediately, with his permission, I ordered a forty-eight pounder to be brought up from a neighbouring

battery and I placed it with so much exactness — having long studied the art of gunnery — that I was sure of my target.

I continued to watch the enemy till I saw the match placed at the touch-hole of their cannon, and at that very instant I gave the signal for our gun to be fired. The guns roared; there was just a moment's pause, and then about midway between the two cannons the cannon balls struck each other with amazing force, and the effect was astonishing! The enemy's cannon ball was knocked back with such violence that it killed the man who had discharged it, by carrying his head off, together with sixteen others which it met with on its way to the Barbary Coast. There, after passing through the masts of three vessels that lay in a line behind each other in the harbour, it broke its way through the roof of a workman's hut, about two hundred yards inland, and destroyed the remaining teeth belonging to an old woman who lay asleep in the hut lying on her back with her mouth open. The ball stuck in her throat.

Soon afterwards, her husband came home and tried to extract the cannon ball. Finding that impossible, with the help of a hammer he knocked it into her stomach, from whence it was discharged downwards in the natural way.

Our cannon ball did excellent service, for it not only repelled the other cannon ball in the way I have just described, but — continuing as I intended it should do — it knocked over the cannon that had just been used against us and forced it into the hold of the ship, where it fell with so much force that it burst its way through the bottom. The ship immediately filled and sank, with more than a thousand Spanish sailors on board and a considerable number of soldiers.

This certainly was an extraordinary exploit. I will not, however, take all the credit; my judgement and knowledge were mainly responsible for our success but I was also helped by chance, for I afterwards discovered that the man who loaded our forty-eight pounder put in, by mistake, a double quantity of gunpowder, without which we could never have succeeded so well, especially in repelling the enemy's cannon ball.

General Elliot wanted to give me a commission for this remarkable piece of service, but I refused everything except his thanks, which he gave me formally in front of his officers at supper that evening.

from *The Adventures of Baron Munchausen* by R. E. Raspe

2. Write a story in which the storyteller exaggerates or distorts what happened to him or her in order to entertain the listeners. It might be the sort of story which a comedian might tell and which an audience would **enjoy** disbelieving.

PERFORMERS

Olga

Most successful and famous performers have to work hard for their success. Here is an account of the daily routine of a famous Russian gymnast and Olympic gold medalist, Olga Korbut, who reached the height of her career while still a teenager.

By eleven o'clock Olga has already put in two hours of solid training in the gymnasium. After this she goes to her college and studies until four, when she returns to her apartment for a late lunch. Then it is training again, three hours of it, from six to nine. It is not until she has completed this that she thinks of taking any relaxation. Bed comes early by Western standards, around ten-thirty, after supper.

Olga needs her eight or nine hours sleep. For six days a week she maintains the regimen. Only on Sundays may she spend the whole day relaxing. If the weather is good, she indulges her favourite pastime, walking in the forests that surround Grodno. Olga's likes and dislikes are simple. After the forest she has always loved dolls. Her preferred mascot is a little hedgehog with purple hair. 'I like this because it smells of sweets,' she says. But the important thing is her training: five hours, every day.

Then there is the other Olga, a different Olga from the Russian student, an Olga who has fan-mail, even if it is addressed simply 'Olga, Moscow' and has been mailed from the other side of the world, that reaches her in vast quantities every morning. This is the Olga who tours. In the year following the Olympic Games she went with the Soviet team to Denmark, Germany, England and the United States. In every city that was visited, there was no doubt about who was the star attraction – Olga. At home too she has a special role to play, and her normal routine is always liable to an unusual variation. Not only does she have to devote time to the special preparations needed for an important gymnastics competition, but she has to meet her fans from the Ukraine, from the Eastern Plains and from all other parts of the Soviet Union. She is constantly invited to visit schools, colleges, factories, military camps and other Russian institutions where she has to give talks describing the performances of her fellow Soviet sportsmen and women at the Olympics, and demonstrate her own skills.

from *Olga* by Justin Beecham

* What would you like and dislike about this sort of life, do you think? What effect would it have on your family and friends? What effect might it have on you?

* Would you feel that in this kind of life you were being deprived of important things?

1. Write a story about a teenage boy or girl whose life is completely changed when he or she becomes a star performer. Your story could be written from the teenager's point of view or from the point of view of a member of his or her family.

* Should children who show particular talent be given special training to develop their talents even if this treatment sets them apart from others of their own age?

* Would you rather be a gifted amateur performer or a world-famous professional?

*. Successful sportsmen and women often have to retire early in their lives. What difficulties might such people have in coming to terms with this?

Fame

Barry John was a remarkable rugby player who retired from the game at the height of his success in the early 1970s. In this extract from his autobiography he explains some of his reasons for quitting the game.

I became famous and I must admit that I liked it – up to a point. But people began to put me on a pedestal and writers started calling me 'a legend in his own lifetime' – a phrase that gave me the creeps, perhaps because it seemed to wrap me up and file me away. I had no wish to be a legend; I wanted to be me. I am a perfectly ordinary individual from an ordinary background.

Let me make myself clear: I don't want to sound ungrateful or selfish or arrogant and I don't want to upset anyone. Rugby has helped me enormously and has given my life a fabulous dimension. After all, I was a teacher and I enjoyed teaching, but I could not have lived the life I do today, even in the purely material sense, on a teacher's salary. Rugby has given me many things, people have done much for me and the rugby ball has certainly bounced very kindly for me.

But, boy, has it brought pressures.

At first it was all fun. What boy wouldn't be tickled at the sight of his name in the local paper? And it was there almost every week in the *Carmarthen Journal* when I played for Cefneithin and Llanelli. It was fun when I began playing for Wales. But in the last year of my playing career, and particularly when I got back from New Zealand, the pressures became more than I could stand.

When I got home the invitations came in thick and fast: to dinners, lunches, meetings, parties, receptions, all kinds of social events. The former simplicity of my life was suddenly altered. I dislike disappointing people and I knew that I owed the Welsh rugby supporters an unpayable debt for their goodwill and support and, in this time of great triumph for Welsh rugby, I felt a duty to go out and meet as many people as possible.

But somehow, in some mysterious metamorphosis, I had been changed from a rugby player into a star.

There was an endless round of personal appearances and I had invitations from societies, clubs and organisations of all kinds, about thirty invitations a week. I even had one from a budgerigar society!

My home life began to suffer and I became a lodger in my own house, darting in to put on a clean shirt before hurrying off to the next engagement. To an extent my wife and little daughter became strangers. Jan said to me several times: 'Why don't you talk to me any more?' But I hardly knew what she meant.

I was getting home at one or two o'clock in the morning, going off to do a day's work and then spending the evening at a function.

Eventually I grew to loathe talking about rugby. I developed the knack of giving an after-dinner type of speech to suit any kind of occasion, but after that I did not want to discuss the game. Everywhere I went people buttonholed me and brought up the hated subject – 'How did you get that penalty? That try? What was X like?' – endless inanities.

I began to scream inwardly. I craved conversation about other topics and I was grateful to the few people who, when they approached for a chat, steered clear of rugby.

I began to feel guilty that this was my reaction. Taking part in small-talk I could hear the words leaving my lips, but they were processed and said without feeling. I began to feel I was cheating people, that I did not care, that I was dishonest and that I had been turned into a kind of circus act.

It began to worry me that the adulation was alienating me from the human race. In a crowd at the National Eisteddfod I was talking to people when I heard a mother tell her small son to touch my hand. Well, I suppose that is a compliment, but I am not a god or a prince or a healer, but a man.

Occasionally I had the curious sensation of not being in my own body, of looking at it as if it were some kind of robot. I was Barry John the rugby star and machine; the real Barry John had stepped outside for a while. In the year up to my retirement from the game I saw my doctor more times than in all the other years of my life put together. And I got into the habit of having a few drinks late at night as a drug to get me off to sleep.

The demands were unbearable. Leaving rugby had nothing to do with the game itself – the very thought or playing a match made my blood race just as it did when I was a schoolboy.

But family life had become impossible and I could not have continued leading this kind of life for many more months. I would have been doing no justice to myself, to my family, my firm, the Welsh team, or the devoted followers of Welsh rugby. In the end I would have let everyone down.

from *The Barry John Story* – an autobiography

* What advantages did Barry John get from being famous and admired?

* Have you ever had your name in the local paper for an achievement? What effect did this have on you and on other people?

* What effects were the pressures of fame having on Barry John's health and his family life?

* 'The demands were unbearable.' What demands is Barry John talking about? Why were they unbearable?

* Barry John says this of himself:
   'people began to put me on a pedestal',
   'the words leaving my lips were processed and said without feeling',
   'the adulation was alienating me from the human race',
   'I had the curious sensation of not being in my own body'.
What did he fear that was happening to him?

* 'But somehow . . . I had been changed from a rugby player into a star.'
   What do you think is the difference between a rugby player – or any other sort of performer – and a star?

* Was he right to give up rugby? Could it be argued that a man with his extraordinary talent for playing rugby and for bringing pleasure into the lives of thousands of people ought to continue to do so?

* If Barry John, or someone like him, was a member of your family, how would you have felt about his decision to retire?

* Whose fault was it that Barry John felt he had to retire from a game he loved at the height of his career?
   Should he have been stronger?
   Should the public demand less of its heroes and stars?
   Are the pressures that accompany fame something that all successful performers should **expect** to have to cope with?

A Way of Life

Sometimes successful performers find it hard to retire, even if they have stopped enjoying success. Here, Tony Palmer writes about a famous pop singer of the 1960s, Dusty Springfield.

Her one ambition became to get out. She felt herself to be an 'article which has to be sold'. Meeting some old school chums of hers recently she said: 'How I envy them. They seem so content.' She became obsessed by her unbeauty. She took to wearing dark stockings to cover up varicose veins and lumpy legs. She retreated behind neon-sign make-up and innumerable blond wigs – lacquered into immobility. She was hopelessly shortsighted, but too vain or proud to wear spectacles. Her Catholic upbringing had brought a certain moral high-mindedness – she refused to perform before segregated audiences in South Africa. She detested loneliness, but after an unhappy series of relationships, she preferred for a while to live alone – alone, that is, except for her constant companion called Einstein whom she discovered one day sitting sadly in a junk-shop. Einstein is a teddy bear. She had wanted to quit but admitted: 'Just what *do* you do when you stop being a pop singer?'

from *Born Under a Bad Sign* by Tony Palmer

* If a friend of yours from school became a famous performer, would you believe it if that person said that he or she envied you your more ordinary life?

* 'Just what **do** you do when you stop being a pop singer?' Can you offer any answers or advice?

Many performers genuinely live for the moments of performance:

I can't express myself in easy conversation – the words just don't come out right. But when I get up on a stage – well, that's my whole life.

Jimi Hendrix from *Born Under a Bad Sign* by Tony Palmer

1. Write a story about someone who gives up being a successful performer. In the story you can create your own imaginary star who quits because of age, or because of the pressures of fame, or because of illness, or for some other reason.

What do you think?

Performers, whether they are actors, musicians, sports players, entertainers or whatever, do what they do for its own sake: fame is irrelevant.

Performers only work hard to improve their skills **in order** to become successful and famous.

The press, radio and television put too much pressure on successful performers: they are hounded everywhere they go. Who wants to know what a pop star thinks about marriage or what a sports player has for breakfast, anyway?

It is a scandal that any performer should be paid more than the Prime Minister.

Famous performers shouldn't expect to be able to have private lives: they must have known what they were letting themselves in for when they started.

1. Write an essay in which you point out the advantages and disadvantages of fame and success. Try to persuade your reader to be sympathetic **or** unsympathetic towards famous performers who resent the pressures that fame has brought.

It's Not What You Say . . .

* You can change the meaning or tone of what you say by altering the way you say it but without changing the words themselves. For example, notice what happens to the sentence — **I shan't be here tomorrow** — if you say it in different ways, emphasising different parts of the sentence:

I shan't be here tomorrow
I **shan't** be here tomorrow
I shan't **be** here tomorrow
I shan't be **here** tomorrow
I shan't be here **tomorrow**
I shan't be here tomorrow?
I shan't be here tomorrow!

You can also produce many more variations by changing the *mood* of the speaker. Try saying the same sentence as if you were —

frightened, nervous, tearful, angry, pleased, upset, defiant, cool, sad . . .

* Working with a partner, see how many different ways you can find of saying these:

It was open
I shall go today
Now
I knew it would happen
Is that really yours
Yes
Please sit down
Sorry
We're moving to Liverpool
We all know what happened then, and we know who we have to thank for what has happened since

* Here is a conversation. Try reading it in as many different ways as you can, changing the mood of the characters and the way the characters behave towards one another.

A: Your sister says you're going to move to Liverpool.
B: Yeah.
A: When are you moving?
B: Next month.
A: Are you going to live in the city?
B: No. We're going to be living right out in the country.
A: Are you pleased?
B: What do you think?

A: What about your brother Andrew?
B: What about him?
A: He's got a job here, hasn't he?
B: Yeah.
A: Will he stay, then?
B: He says he's getting a flat.
A: You'll be able to come back here to say, then, if you want.
B: Oh yeah. Great.

* In order to present or perform speeches in plays, actors have to try out many different ways of expressing the words. They try to find the way that suits them and suits their view of the characters they play and the situations and moods of the scenes they appear in.

Read the speech below:

> I was just walking along the street, minding my own business. It was Saturday afternoon. Lots of people about, you know. Very busy. I remember I'd just decided I'd go into Marks and Sparks for a quick look round.
>
> Well, I'd just got in, through the swing doors. There was a bit of a crush, and I held one of them open for this woman with a baby. Well, it just happened – just like that. No warning at all. First I was going in, holding back the door, then –!!
>
> It took some time to get over it. I don't mean just then, at that moment (although it was bad enough at the time). No, I mean later on, when things got more sorted out. Even now. I think about it a lot, even now.

Try performing this speech in different ways, with different people in mind. Decide what happened, and to whom. Is the speech spoken by someone who is laughing, or angry, or resentful, or self-pitying, for example?

Is it a man or a woman talking? A teenage boy or girl? A young mother? An elderly person?

Should there be some slight changes in the wording to suit the character you have in mind? Try changing details if you think it necessary, and then continue the speech.

First Night

The leading actor, Alec McCowen, describes his feelings on the day of the opening performance of a new play – in this case Hadrian VII *at the Mermaid Theatre in London.*

A first night, of course, includes the day that leads up to the performance, and the whole chaos that goes on after it.

I get up in the morning and go through the everyday routines of bathing, shaving, dressing, drinking coffee – as if for the very last time. It is impossible to imagine the existence of tomorrow.

If I have been given the day off and I perhaps do some shopping for first-night cards and presents, a sudden twinge of fatigue will frighten me into believing that I have already used up the evening's strength. And the casual behaviour of shop-keepers, taxi-drivers and the general populace seems heartless and cruel as I nurse my private terror of the exposure to come.

If I stay at home I might lie down and try to rest – soon discovering that, in addition to holding my breath, my body is suspended one inch above the bed.

I get up and play a noisy gramophone record until I fear that I'm being emotionally drained and hurriedly switch off.

Finally, when I leave home to go to the theatre, I often say goodbye to my image in the mirror – as if the horror of the evening may actually change my appearance beyond recognition.

Most directors call the company in to the theatre for a rehearsal in the afternoon – simply to give everyone something to do. 'We won't rehearse properly,' they say. 'Just run through some of the lines. Don't strain your voice or tire yourselves.'

So you rehearse – improperly – without straining your voice or tiring yourselves, and immediately start to dry up and wonder whether you've forgotten the whole play.

Your dressing-room is full of telegrams from friends, and cards and little gifts from the company. You realise guiltily that you've forgotten several people in the cast – and *always* the designer.

Soon there are little taps on the door and people wish you luck – as if they are saying goodbye for the last time. Worst of all are the producers, who are usually more nervous than the actors, since they have nothing to do but sit out front and watch. You try to soothe them, and wish they'd go away. Often the stage-management give you helpful last-minute titbits of information such as, 'The paint's still wet on the mantelpiece', or 'We've lost the newspaper you read in Act Two', and nearly always, 'I'm sorry but that door's still sticking'.

Alec McCowen dressed for his part in the play *Hadrian VII*

You touch up your make-up for the tenth time – and then realise you look like a silent film star and rub it all off again.

They call the five minutes and add the information that the curtain will go up ten minutes late – so you have at least another fifteen minutes to kill.

You resist the temptation to go down to the stage, and start to pester the other members of the cast by knocking at their doors and wishing *them* luck.

You return to your room and check your quick changes, and look at the script to find the first thing you ever wrote in it.

I wonder if I have enough drinks and glasses for visitors after the show.

I wonder if anyone will come round after the show.

I wonder if I'll still be alive after the show.

I wonder – 'Beginners, please!'

Edith Evans, on being wished good luck before a performance replied, 'I don't need luck. I need application.'

I think you need both.

Because there is no curtain at the Mermaid Theatre, before the play started I used to sit on the stage in the dark in my little room – which was built on a revolving truck – and listen to the audience chattering. When everyone was in, the stage-manager gave the cue to dim the house-lights, and two young stage-hands, dressed in black habits like monks, used to push the revolving truck round. The lights came up to discover me sitting in my chair writing my book, until the landlady, Mrs Crowe, played by Margaret Courtenay, knocked at the door.

'Mr Rolfe! Mr Rolfe!'

And we were off!

from *Double Bill* Alec McCowen

* Alec McCowen says it is 'impossible to imagine the existence of tomorrow' (that is, the day after the first performance). Have you ever felt the same before an important event?

* What does Alec McCowen mean when he says, 'my body is suspended one inch above the bed'?

* Why should the producers be more nervous than the actors?

* Edith Evans (a distinguished actress of her time) said you don't need luck before a performance, you need application (or hard work and concentration). Which do **you** think is more important?

* As a professional actor, Alec McCowen will experience several first nights each year. Since he obviously finds them very upsetting experiences, why does he continue to perform, do you think?

1. Imagine you have to face an important test of your abilities or skills or strength in the next twenty-four hours: it might be a race, a play, an interview, an examination, an operation, a sports match, an audition, a concert . . . Write about your feelings and experiences leading up to the event.

The Entertainment

Laurie Lee looks back on a village concert which he took part in. First there was tea in the village hall and then came the Entertainment.
Young Laurie waits anxiously for his performance to begin.

We crowded outside and huddled in the snow while the tables were taken away. Inside, behind curtains, the actors were making up – and my moment, too, was approaching. The snow whirled about me and I began to sweat, I wanted to run off home. Then the doors reopened and I crouched by the stove, shivering and chattering with nerves. The curtains parted and the Entertainment began with a comic I neither saw nor heard . . .

'For the next item, ladies and gentlemen, we have an instrumental duet, by Miss Brown and – er – young Laurie Lee.'

Smirking with misery I walked to the stage. Eileen's face was as white as
10 a minim. She sat at the piano, placed the music crooked, I straightened it, it fell to the ground. I groped to retrieve it; we looked at one another with hatred; the audience was still as death. Eileen tried to give me an A, but struck B instead, and I tuned up like an ape threading needles. At last we were ready, I raised my fiddle; and Eileen was off like a bolting horse. I caught her up in the middle of the piece – which I believe was a lullaby – and after playing the repeats, only twice as fast, we just stopped, frozen motionless, spent.

Some hearty stamping and whistling followed, and a shout of 'Give us another!' Eileen and I didn't exchange a glance, but we loved each other
20 now. We found the music of 'Danny Boy' and began to give it all our emotion, dawdling dreamily among the fruitier chords and scampering over the high bits; till the audience joined in, using their hymn-singing voices, which showed us the utmost respect. When it was over I returned to my seat by the stove, my body feeling smooth and beautiful. Eileen's mother was weeping into her hat, and so was mine, I think . . .

Now I was free to become one of the audience, and the Entertainment burgeoned before me. What had seemed to me earlier as the capering of demons now became a spectacle of human genius. Turn followed turn in variety and splendour.

30 Major Doveton came next, with his Indian banjo, which was even harder to tune than my fiddle. He straddled a chair and began wrestling with the keys, cursing us in English and Urdu. Then all the strings broke, and he snarled off the stage and started kicking the banjo round the cloakroom. He was followed by a play in which Marjorie, as Cinderella, sat in a goose-feathered dress in a castle. While waiting for the pumpkin to turn into a coach, she sang 'All alone by the telephone'.

from *Cider with Rosie* by Laurie Lee

* What tells us that Laurie is nervous about his performance?

* How can we tell that Laurie is relieved when his performance is over?

1. Look back on one of your own performances: in sport; using words; demonstrating. Try to write about your feelings before, during and after the performance, as Laurie Lee does.

2. Major Doveton's performance went badly wrong. Can you remember any occasion when you had to perform in public or in a classroom or before friends or relations, and things went wrong? Describe what happened.

* This is a description of an amateur entertainment in which some of the performers are not very talented, and yet the audience obviously enjoyed it, and Laurie Lee has remembered it. Is taking part in a performance as best you can more important than performing to a high standard, do you think, or should we only applaud the very best and only perform if we are gifted?

A Closer Look

1. Why does Entertainment begin with a capital E? (line 6)

2. Why does Laurie Lee mention 'snow' and 'sweat' together, and crouching 'by the stove' and 'chattering with nerves', together? (lines 3 to 5)

3. 'Smirking with misery I walked to the stage.' (line 9) How can someone smirk (or smile) with misery?

4. 'Eileen's face was white as a minim.' (lines 9 to 10)
'the audience was still as death'. (line 12)
How many comparisons can you find in this paragraph? How do they give force to the writing?

5. Why does Laurie Lee include the description of the duet 'which I believe was a lullaby'? (lines 15 to 16)

6. Compare the shape and length of sentences in the paragraph beginning, 'Smirking with misery' with the shape and length of those in the next paragraph. What differences do you notice? What is the effect of these differences?

7. Why do two paragraphs end with three dots instead of one full stop?

Scenes from 'Cooper's Lodge'

Work in a group of three or four. Read this scene (which is the first scene from the play, *Cooper's Lodge*) several times, working towards a performance of it. You may find it useful to let more than one person in the group have a go at each part.

In order to perform this scene convincingly, you have to work out the mood and state of mind of each character and how he or she feels about other characters in the scene. Try reading the speeches in different ways until the group is satisfied with one reading. Here are some questions to help you:

> Are the characters excited? Are they pleased? frightened? nervous? calm? upset? angry? friendly to one another? worried? comforting? happy? tense? sulky? sullen? bored? defensive? aggressive? hysterical? amused? sympathetic? sarcastic?

Each character can, of course, be in more than one state of mind during a single scene, and the feelings one character has towards another can change during a conversation.

Two boys from Manchester, Stephen and David, are sitting in the front seats of a car. They are dressed in jeans and anoraks. It is winter. We hear the sound of the car being driven at speed.

David :	Fantastic! Goes like a bomb!
Stephen :	What?
David :	Like a bomb!
Stephen :	You reckon?
David :	Better than my old man's, at any rate.
Stephen :	Ever driven one of these before?
David :	Drove a 1300 once. Not much difference.
Stephen :	Get on!
David :	I'm right! This is just bigger, that's all.
Stephen :	What are we doing?
David :	Sixty. About that.
Stephen :	What would she do, d'you think, if you really opened her up?
David :	Ton; maybe a bit more.
Stephen :	D'you reckon?
David :	Wait till we're out of this twisty bit, and I'll show you.
Stephen :	What's up ahead: that light?
David :	Cross Keys, I think. Fancy a drink?
Stephen :	No! We'd get copped!
David :	You were keen enough earlier on.
Stephen :	What d'you mean?
David :	Ah, skip it!
Stephen :	Too late now, anyway. What's that?
David :	What?
Stephen :	Up ahead.
David :	Get out of the road you stupid –
	(*The noise of the car's horn drowns his voice*)
Stephen :	He's drunk! Look out! He's staggering out!
	(*There is a squeal of tyres*)
	You hit him!
David :	Shut up! Shut up, will you?
Stephen :	You hit him, Dave!
David :	I didn't, he'll be all right!
Stephen :	You did! What if he's – what if he's hurt?
David :	We only touched him; he'll be all right.
Stephen :	Slow down, slow down for God's sake!
David :	Get off me!
Stephen :	Slow down, there's a corner.
David :	Get off! Get off the wheel!
Stephen :	Stop! Stop it! Stop the car!
David :	Get off the wheel!
	(*We hear the sound of the car going off the road and coming to a sudden halt. Silence for a moment or two*)

In your groups also prepare a performance of the following two scenes from the same play, using the same techniques as you used for the first scene.

The boys are frightened by what they have done. They decide to go away for a few days, walking and staying in youth hostels in North Wales. They are not used to hiking, and in their hurry to get away they go without proper equipment or clothing. They are caught in a blizzard and have to shelter in an old shepherd's hut which has been turned into a refuge for climbers. Here they settle down for an uncomfortable night . . .

	(*Above the noise of the wind, we hear a sudden bang outside the door. Both boys are startled*)
Stephen :	What's that?
David :	There's something outside!
Stephen :	There can't be! Sh!
	(*The door bursts open and two figures enter, dressed in kagouls, and well-protected against the weather. They carry haversacks and bed-rolls. Although these two are, in fact, Christine and Anne, it is impossible in the dark and because of their clothing, to tell this. They push the door to behind them. One of them flashes a torch around the room*)
David :	Who are you? What do you want?
Christine :	We didn't expect –
Stephen :	It's a couple of birds!
David :	What do you want?
Christine :	Obvious, isn't it? We're sheltering from the weather.
Stephen :	What, here?
Anne :	Looks like it, doesn't it? Can we come in, please?
David :	I thought you already were.
Anne :	I mean do you mind if we put our stuff down?
Stephen :	Be our guest. Make yourselves at home.
Christine :	Wait a minute, Anne. I've got a lantern here.
David :	Is it just you two? Or is it a coach trip?
Christine :	No, there's just me and Anne.
Stephen :	What's your name then?
Christine :	Christine.
David :	Chris.
Christine :	No. Christine.
David :	Sorry, I'm *sure*. I'm Dave, and that's Steve.
Christine :	Where shall I put this? (*referring to the lantern*)
David :	Put it on that ledge. You want it as high as you can.
	(*Christine puts the lantern on the ledge and lights the lamp*)
Christine :	There, that's better.
	(*They look round at one another, smile shyly*)

David: Did you get caught in the blizzard?

Anne: Yes, we thought we'd better stop here.

Stephen: Did you know this place was here then?

Christine: Yes, it's on the map.

Anne: Didn't you know that?

Stephen: No, we just sort of stumbled across it.

Christine: Haven't you got a map?

David: (*joking*) No, but I've got a built-in compass in here. (*taps his head*)

Christine: You ought to have a map.

Stephen: There are a lot of things we ought to have –

David: I've got a wonderful sense of direction, but a lousy memory.

Anne: How long have you been here?

David: Oh, we come here for our holiday every year.

Anne: No, really.

Stephen: We came in this afternoon. (*to David*) I thought you were freezing cold a minute ago.

David: I am still. (*starts putting on his second pair of trousers*)

Christine: I see you've got the fire going. That's something.

David: Gee, thanks.

Cooper's Lodge

Christine :	(*ignores the remark*) Can you just shove round a bit so we can put these wet things out?
Stephen :	You look like you've come from Antarctica.
David :	Hey, don't forget I'm the one who's supposed to be cold.
Christine :	Sorry, but we must get these dry. (*moves David's training shoes*) You haven't been walking in these have you?
David :	What's it to you?
Anne :	I've got some spare socks here. Would they help?
David :	Yeah, thanks.
Stephen :	Jammy devil!
Christine :	Have you come far today?
David :	About three or four miles I reckon, just up from the valley.
Anne :	Where were you going?
David :	To the youth hostel.
Anne :	Which one?
David :	That one at the top of the valley. There was a map by the bus stop.
Christine :	You mean the one near the dam on the reservoir.
David :	Yes, that's it—
Stephen :	You're bulling. He hasn't a clue where we are.
David :	Nor have you.
Stephen :	Who's pretending?
Christine :	But you're miles from any hostel!
David :	Well, so what? What about you?
Christine :	But we know where we are, exactly. (*She looks round*) I've passed here before.
Anne :	Are those socks all right?
David :	Yes thanks, great.
Anne :	Only you must keep warm. You mustn't get hypothermia.
David :	What's that, junkies' disease? (*He pretends to inject his arm*)
Anne :	No, it's when you get too cold.
Christine :	Oh Anne, he's not that cold. Are you?
David :	(*joking*) Tell me the worst doctor. I can take it.
Christine :	He'll be all right.
Stephen :	Are you two on holiday?
Christine :	Sort of.
Anne :	We're doing an award scheme. It's a weekend hike.
David :	You mean you do this because you like it?
Anne :	Well, we—
Christine :	Of course we do.
Stephen :	You must be mad.
Christine :	Well what about you, then?
Stephen :	We just wanted to get away for a couple of days.
David :	'Get away from it all' You know! the pressure, the fans—!
Stephen :	— groupies, booze, fast cars.

Anne:	Like hell.
David:	I'll take you for a joy ride any day.
Anne:	Oh thanks.
David:	I mean it. If you play your cards right.
Christine:	You aren't even old enough.
David:	So?

Later the group settles down to sleep . . .

Anne:	It's very bad out there.
Stephen:	It's not exactly draught-proof in here. Hey, Dave, a bit of a contrast between last night and this.
David:	You can say that again.
	(*Stephen makes the sound of a car passing at speed*)
Christine:	Be quiet! I don't want to hear about your little adventures.
	(*Stephen repeats the noise*)
David:	She said be quiet!
Christine:	I wish you'd both shut up. I want to get some sleep.
Stephen:	Yes miss (*He settles to sleep*)

(*The lights dim to blackness, the sound of the wind increases. Pause. We hear the sound of a car moving at speed as at the beginning of the play. The car's tyres screech and we hear the vehicle going off the road. During this we hear David:*)

David:	Get out of the road! Get out of the road! Get off the wheel!
	(*When the noise is at its loudest it stops suddenly. The light of a cold dawn appears through the window. Christine crouches at David's side, gently shaking him. He is still muttering*)
Christine:	Dave! David! What's the matter? Wake up!
David:	Get out of the road! (*He wakes*) Oh!
Christine:	What's the matter? You were dreaming.
David:	Oh. Yes. Was I talking?
Christine:	You were shouting.
David:	It must be this floor. It's cold. What did I say?
Christine:	You kept saying, 'Get out of the road' or something.
David:	Did I wake you up?
Christine:	Yes.
David:	Sorry.
Christine:	It's all right. What were you dreaming about?
David:	Nothing. I can't sleep properly on here.
Christine:	Do you have nightmares?
David:	No. Not specially.
Christine:	Something about a wheel. What was it?
David:	I thought you weren't interested in my little adventures.
Christine:	Oh, I see.
David:	It was just something that happened the other night.
Christine:	You were driving a car.

David :   Yes. Something like that.
Christine :   You don't have a licence, do you?
David :   No. It wasn't exactly my car either.
Christine :   Was it your dad's?
David :   No. I 'borrowed' it.
Christine :   You really think you're great, don't you?
David :   Maybe I am.
Christine :   And maybe you're not. I suppose you crashed it.
David :   Well, sort of bent it a bit.
Christine :   Was Steve with you?
David :   Yeah, my heroic friend. If it hadn't been for him, we wouldn't have come off the road in the first place.
Christine :   What did he do?
David :   He pulled the wheel and we went into the ditch. He panicked.
Christine :   So is that why you're up here?
David :   It seemed a good idea; sort of fade out for a day or two.
Christine :   Out of the frying pan, into the fire.
David :   Some fire.
Christine :   It's still snowing.
David :   Yes.
Christine :   It can't go on for ever.
David :   I expect it'll try.
Christine :   Were you dreaming about the car crash?
David :   No.
Christine :   Well, what then?
David :   The crash doesn't matter.
Christine :   You don't care about anything, do you? You don't give a damn.
David :   Thanks.
Christine :   Will you be warm enough?
            (*David snores deliberately in order to snub her. She shrugs and returns to her sleeping bag and the lights fade. The storm continues*)

            Later that morning . . .
David :   These shoes are all right now. They're dry.
Christine :   They won't last long.
David :   They're good shoes, these!
Christine :   It depends what you mean by 'good'.
            (*Stephen enters, picks up the radio. He turns it on*)
Stephen :   All right if I take this?
            (*They ignore him. The music fades as he goes out*)
Christine :   He seems cheerful enough.
David :   He's short on imagination, Steve.
Christine :   How do you mean?

David:	Oh, I don't know. He never gets upset unless something bad's actually happening. Me, I get worried about things that are *going* to happen.
Christine:	What sort of things?
David:	Going to the dentist; waiting for me dad to find out about something I've done.
Christine:	I know what you mean. I think I do, anyway.
David:	Huh!
Christine:	What's that supposed to mean?
David:	Nowt. Forget it.
Christine:	I'm sorry if I wasn't very sympathetic.
David:	When?
Christine:	Last night. About the accident.
David:	Oh, that, yeah.
Christine:	It's just that, last night, you didn't seem bothered about crashing that car.
David:	He can get another one, it'll be insured.
Christine:	That's awful! That's not the point!
David:	Why not?
Christine:	Suppose it was your car? How would you feel?
David:	It *wasn't* my car.
Christine:	But if it was?
David:	If, if, if—.
Christine:	If it had been your car, you'd have been really angry.
David:	It's only a heap of tin. It's the bloke I worry about.
Christine:	Well, that's who I'm talking about: the owner.
David:	Not him; the other one.
Christine:	Who?
David:	The other man; the one in the road; the one we hit!
Christine:	You what?
	(*Stephen enters with the radio to his ear. They stand apart awkwardly. Stephen is oblivious of the atmosphere. He lounges on his bed-roll*)
Stephen:	Do you reckon Presley was any good?
David:	What? Oh, er, yes. 'Course he was.
Stephen:	I reckon he's rubbish. (*He continues to listen*)
Christine:	Someone in a car?
David:	No, he was walking. He might have been drunk.
Christine:	And you knocked him down.
David:	I suppose so. We hit him.
Christine:	You didn't stop?
David:	No. Well, not till we crashed.
Christine:	Why didn't you stop?
David:	Dunno. Scared, I suppose.

Christine :	You should have stopped. You have to stop.
David :	Well, we didn't. Not until *he* pulled the wheel.
Christine :	Did he try to stop you then?
David :	No, he was just scared. We both were.
Christine :	But did you hit him hard? How fast were you going?
David :	Fast enough. Steve said he went flying.
Christine :	Wasn't there anybody around?
David :	I don't think so. It was dark.
Christine :	So he might have been left there ages. On the road.
David :	He could've been.
Christine :	What are you going to do?
David :	What would you do?
Christine :	I'd have stopped.
David :	Are you sure?
Christine :	Well I know I wouldn't have cleared off.
David :	You don't know what you'd do.
Christine :	What'll happen? Will they find out?
David :	They might. I don't see how; they've nothing to go on.
Christine :	It wasn't very bright to come up here; you'll just draw attention to yourselves.
David :	Well, maybe I'm not very bright. We can't all be Brain of Britain.
Christine :	I think it stinks!
David :	Well how the hell would you know? I bet you've never been in any trouble!

from *Cooper's Lodge* by G. Sanderson and C. R. Beecroft

* When you have thoroughly prepared the scenes, perform them. You may choose to present the scenes as part of a radio play.

* The first scene takes place in a car which is moving at 60 mph. The car crashes and goes off the road. How would you stage this scene?

1. Try to write the scene or scenes which might follow these extracts. Perhaps you can bring the play to its conclusion. Compare your version of what might happen with the writing of others in the class and discuss which ideas you find most convincing.

The Actor

Albert Royston is the assistant manager of a large grocery store. He is persuaded to play the part of a policeman in an amateur play. He is very nervous about this, his first-ever performance.

He was at the hall early on the night of the play and made up and dressed in the police constable's uniform by the end of the first act. As the second act began he found himself alone in the dressing-room. He looked into the mirror and squared the helmet on his head. He certainly looked the part all right. It would be a bit of a lark to go out in the street and pinch somebody for speeding or something. He narrowed his eyes, looking fiercely at himself, and spoke his opening line in a gutteral undertone.

Well, this was it. No good looking in the book. If he didn't know the part now he never would. Out there the second act was under way, the players doing their very best, revelling in a hobby they loved, giving entertainment to all those people; and in return the audience was thrilling to every twist and climax of the plot, and not letting one witty phrase, one humorous exchange go by without a laugh. A good audience, Mrs Bostock had said: the sort of audience all actors, professional or amateur, loved: at one with the players, receptive, responsive, appreciative. And soon its eyes would be on him.

He was suddenly seized by an appalling attack of stage fright. His stomach was empty, a hollow void of fear. He put his head in his hands. He couldn't do it. How could he have ever imagined he could? He couldn't face all those people. His mouth was dry and when he tried to bring his lines to memory he found nothing but a blank.

A knock on the door made him look up. He felt panic grip him now. Had he missed his entrance? Had he ruined the performance for everybody by cringing here like a frightened child? The knock was repeated and Mrs Bostock's voice said from outside, 'Are you there, Mr Royston?'

Albert took his script in his hand and opened the door. She smiled brightly up at him. 'Everything all right?' She gave him an appraising look. 'You look wonderful. You're not on for a little while yet but I should come and stand in the wings and get the feel of the action. You look a bit pale about the gills. What's wrong – stage fright?'

'It's all a bit new to me,' Albert said feebly.

'Of course it is. But you know your lines perfectly and once you're out there you'll forget your nervousness. Just remember the audience is on your side.'

They went up the narrow steps to the level of the stage. The voices of the actors became more distinct. He caught the tail-end of a line he recognised. There already? Recurrent fear gripped his stomach.

He looked out onto the brightly lit stage, at the actors moving about, talking, and across to where the girl who was acting as prompter sat with an open script on her knee. 'Shirley hasn't had a thing to do so far,' Mrs Bostock murmured 'The whole thing's gone like a dream.' She took the script from Albert's hands and found the place for him. 'Here we are. Now you just follow the action in there and relax, take it easy. You'll be on and off so quick you'll hardly know you've left the wings.'

'I'm all right now,' Albert told her.

He realised to his own surprise that he was; and he became increasingly so as the action of the play absorbed him, so that he began to feel himself part of it and no longer a frightened amateur shivering in the wings.

Two pages to go. The younger son was telling his brother about the accident. The row was just beginning and at the very height of it he would make his entrance. He began to feel excited. What was it Mrs Bostock had said? 'From the second you step on you dominate the stage. Your entrance is like a thunder-clap.' By shots! He realised vaguely that Mrs Bostock had left his side, but he didn't care now. He felt a supreme confidence. He was ready. He'd show them. By shots he would!

One page. ' "You've been rotten all your life, Paul," ' the elder brother was saying. ' "I've never cherished any illusions about you, but this, this is

more than even I dreamed you were capable of." '

' "I know you hate me, Tom. I've always known it. But if only for father's sake, you must help me now. You know what it will do to him if he finds out. He couldn't stand it in his condition." '

' "You swine. You utter swine . . ." '

The girl who was the maid appeared at his side. She gave him a quick smile. No nerves about her. She'd been on and off the stage all evening, living the part. Albert stared out, fascinated. Not until this moment had he known the true thrill of acting, of submerging one's own personality in that of another.

' "Where are you going?" '

' "I'm going to find that man you knocked down and get him to a hospital. And you're coming with me." '

' "But it's too late, Tom. It was hours ago. Someone's sure to have found him by now. Perhaps the police . . ." '

Any minute now. They were working up to his entrance. *Like a thunderclap.* Albert braced his shoulders and touched his helmet. He glanced down at the script and quickly turned a page. He had lost his place. Panic smote him like a blow. They were still talking, though, so he must be all right. And anyway the maid gave him his cue and she was still by his side. Then suddenly she was no longer at his side. She had gone. He fumbled with his script. Surely . . . not so far . . .

He felt Mrs Bostock at his elbow. He turned to her in stupid surprise. 'But,' he said, 'They're . . . they've –'

She nodded. 'Yes. They've skipped three pages. They've missed your part right out.'

from *The Actor* by Stan Barstow

1. Carry on the story. What would be Albert's feelings after this event?

2. Write a story about yourself involving a disappointing ending to some event which you had been looking forward to very keenly.

∗ What causes stage-fright? How would you help someone try to deal with it?

Missing

Choose one or more of the headlines above and tell the story behind them in the form of a **file**. The file should include such items as:

newspaper reports,
     interviews with parents,
          letters connected with the story,
photographs and pictures,
     extracts from the diary kept by the missing person,
          statements made to the police,
             maps and plans of where the people disappeared . . .

BULLIES

Phyllisia

Phyllisia is a West Indian girl living in Harlem, New York.

Since my father had sent for us, my sister Ruby who is sixteen and me, two years younger, and set us down in this miserable place called Harlem, New York, this was the first warm day. I, too, had not wanted to come here today. Walking to school, seeing people coming out of their homes with faces softened by smiles, for the first time I had been filled with the desire to run off somewhere, anywhere but to this room. I had not wanted to have to listen to a teacher I did not like, nor to sit among children I liked even less. But where could I go? I knew nothing about this strange city. Going one block out of my way between home and school, and I would be lost. And so I had come, grudgingly, but I had come.

Yet the moment I had entered the classroom, I knew that my instincts had been right. I should not have come today. The same recklessness that had pulled at me in the streets was big in the room, pulling and tugging at the control of the students. Fear cut a zigzag pattern from my stomach to my chest: The students in the class did not like *me*.

They mocked my West Indian accent, called me names – 'monkey' was one of the nicer ones. Sometimes they waited after school to tease me, following me at times for several blocks, shouting. But it had been cold and after a time they had been only too glad to hunch their shoulders up to their ears and go home. Winter, as much as I hated it, had protected me. Now it was spring.

Automatically my gaze sought the big-breasted girl sitting diagonally across the room from me – Beulah. Beulah sat with her head bowed down to the desk obviously reading a comic book she had concealed beneath. Beulah was the toughest girl I had ever known. She was so tough that she did anything she wanted to in class, and Miss Lass looked the other way. But the worst of it was that Beulah for some reason *hated* me.

'Come on, let's split this scene,' Edith whispered. 'I got money. We can go to some jazzy place and wait the time out.'

Her words lit my mind with pictures of what she meant by jazzy places – places like parks and lakes and outdoor movies. All I had to do was turn and smile at this dirty little girl and she could take me to places that I had never been to before. But then I thought about Calvin and the brilliant thoughts fizzled out.

Calvin is my father. To myself I use his first name, as a sign of disrespect. The first week we had come, I demanded of him why he had sent for us to set us down in this trap of asphalt and stone called Harlem. 'Because I have the right. To control your rudeness better,' he had said. 'What blame control does he think we need,' I had muttered to my sister

Ruby loud enough for him to hear. The next moment my lips were swelling up from a backhand slap. I had not even seen it coming. '*Who* needs control?' he asked. I sulked at first, refusing to answer. But the next time he said, 'I ask you, who needs control?' I gave one look into his set, black face, with anger burning out of his eyes, and my determination not to answer flickered out. 'Me,' I answered meekly, and my hatred of him mounted.

No, it would not do for Calvin to see me out in the streets when I should be in school. And with someone looking like Edith?

I pulled my attention back into the room just in time to hear Miss Lass throw a question in my direction.

'Can anyone tell me on what continent the country of Egypt is located?' she asked.

I stared fixedly at the blackboard. While it was certain I could not leave school, it was also certain that I did not feel like standing in the full glare of the children's animosity on this warm touchy day to answer any questions.

Teacher waited. The class waited. I waited, praying someone else would know the answer and, barring that, Miss Lass herself would explain. I did not remember her ever discussing Africa before. But I had been the star pupil too long – always jumping up to let others know how smart I was. And so Miss Lass kept looking at me while I kept looking at the blackboard. Finally, after a few minutes, she called: 'Phyllisia?'

I did not move. Why did she want to make an example of me to the other children? There were at least thirty others she could call on. 'Phyllisia!' I still kept my seat. I kept repeating to myself: I will not stand. I will not answer. I will not.

Then someone snickered, and someone else. My face burned with shame. Sitting there and not answering was like begging. And why should I beg? I had done nothing to anybody. I found myself standing. I heard my voice saying, despite a sixth sense warning me to remain silent, to stay in my seat, 'Egypt is in Africa.' Once started I kept on talking to dispel any notion that I might be guessing. 'It is bordered on the South by the Sudan and on the North by the Mediterranean Sea which opens up into the Nile, which is the longest river in Africa and perhaps the world.'

I resumed my seat, a taste of chalk in my mouth, unsatisfied with the display of my brilliance. Nor did I feel any better at the flurry of shuffling feet, the banging of more desks and the sound of contemptuous whispers.

'No it ain't either,' a boy shouted from the back of the room. 'They got A-rabs in Egypt. Everybody know ain't no A-rabs in Africa.'

'That's where you are wrong,' Miss Lass shrilled. 'Egypt *is* a country in Africa. If some of you would follow Phyllisia's example and study your books, then perhaps the intelligence rate in this room might zoom up to zero.'

I felt a dozen needles sticking in my stomach. I leaned back in my seat. The fingernails of the girl behind me dug into my back. 'Teacher's pet,' she hissed. I pulled away, but as I did my head magnetically turned and I found myself staring into the eyes of the thick-muscled girl with the breasts. She had turned completely around in her seat so that her back faced the teacher while she stared at me. As our stares locked, she balled up her fist, put it first over one eye and then the other. The needles in my stomach multiplied by thousands.

from *The Friends* by Rosa Guy

* With the coming of spring 'people (were) **coming out of their homes with faces softened by smiles'**, but the arrival of warm weather increases the tensions between Phyllisia and her classmates. Why?

* Why does Phyllisia stand up and answer the question about Egypt when she knows it is not wise to do so?
Is she inviting the hatred of the others?
Why does she think that **'Sitting there and not answering was like begging.'**?

* Having read this extract, can you suggest any reasons why most of the class, and Beulah in particular, should resent or hate Phyllisia?

* **'They mocked my West Indian accent, called me names — "monkey" was one of the nicer ones. Sometimes they waited after school to tease me, following me at times for several blocks, shouting.'**
Is this bullying, or racial prejudice, or both, or something else?

* Why doesn't Phyllisia call her father Calvin to his face?

* Discuss the following statements about Phyllisia. How much evidence for each one is there in the extract?

> She is proud.
> She is weak and tame.
> She is brave.
> She is a show-off.
> She is cool.

* Does Phyllisia's father bully her or does she need **'control'**?

* What do you think of what Miss Lass says in praising Phyllisia?

1. Write about a time when you were rejected or made to feel unpopular by other people of your own age. What happened? Whose fault was it? How did you cope with it?

2. Imagine yourself in Phyllisia's position and write about what happens next.

Fight!

Enter Mr Farthing, running. The boys mooching around the fringes of the fight, like supporters locked out of a football ground, spread the word. The word spread amongst the back ranks of the crowd, and the knot slackened as boys hurried away before Mr Farthing could reach them. But at the core of the activity the attention was too fixed to be diverted, and when Mr Farthing forced his way through, dragging boys aside by their arms, their faces turned on him, flicking through the emotions of anger, shock, and finally amusement at the thought of their initial reaction. He lifted MacDowall off Billy and shook him like a terrier shakes a rat. The spectators adjourned to a safer distance. Mr Farthing looked round at them, blazing.

'I'm giving you lot ten seconds to get back round to the yard. If I see one face after that time I'll give its owner the biggest belting he's ever received.'

He started to count. Four seconds later MacDowall's and Billy's faces were the only two in sight.

'Now then what's going off?'

Billy began to cry. MacDowall wiped his nose along the back of one hand and looked down at it.

'Well? . . . Casper?'

'It wa' him, Sir! He started it!'

'I didn't, Sir! It wa' him, he started chucking cokes at me!'

'Ar, what for though?'

'Nowt!'

'You liar!'

Mr Farthing closed his eyes and cancelled all the explanations with a crossed sweep of his arms.

'Shut up. Both of you. It's the same old tale; it's nobody's fault, and nobody started it, you just happened to be fighting on top of a heap of coke for no reason at all. I ought to send you both to Mr Gryce!'

He tossed his head back at the school, and the words came out, ground from between his teeth.

'Just look at the mess you've both made!'

Two dustbins were lying on their sides, their contents spilling out, and three more bins were without their lids. The pile of coke had been trampled into a cokey beach, and odd lumps had been kicked across the asphalt, some into the cycle shed.

'Just look at it! It's disgusting! And just look at the state of you both!'

One lap of MacDowall's shirt curved out from beneath his sweater, and covered one thigh, like half an apron. Billy's shirt buttons had burst open all down the front. One button was missing, the corresponding button-

hole ripped open. Their hair looked as though they had been scratching their scalps solidly for a week, and their faces were the colour of colliers'.

'And stop blubbering, Casper! You're not dying, lad!'

'He will be when I get hold of him.'

Mr Farthing stepped up to MacDowall and bent his knees to bring their faces level.

'You're a brave boyo, aren't you, MacDowall? He's just about your size, isn't he, Casper? Well if you're so keen on fighting, why don't you pick on somebody your own size? Eh? Eh?' simultaneously pushing MacDowall twice in the shoulder.

'Because you're scared, aren't you? Aren't you, MacDowall?' Right jab, right again, stepping up each time MacDowall retreated.

'You're nothing but a bully boy. The classic example of a bully! If it isn't Casper, then it's someone else like him. Isn't it, isn't it, MacDowall?' Jab. Jab.

They left Billy behind, progressing into the shed with halting corresponding steps, like partners learning to dance.

'What would you say if I pinned you to the floor and smacked you across the face?' Jab. Jab.

MacDowall began to sob.

'You'd say I was a bully, wouldn't you lad? And you'd be right, because I'm bigger and stronger, and I know that I could beat you to pulp before we started. Just like you know, MacDowall, with every boy you pick on!' The next two jabs developed into thumps.

'I'll tell my dad!'

'Of course you will, lad. Boys like you always tell their dads. And then do you know what I'll do, MacDowall? I'll tell mine. And then what will happen? Eh?'

MacDowall banged his head on the back of the shed, making the tin rattle. Mr Farthing completed his last step, closing the gap between them again.

'And do you know, MacDowall, that my dad's the heavy-weight champion of the world? So what's going to happen to your dad then. Eh? And what's going to happen to you? Eh? Eh? MacDowall?'

He roared out this last question and stood up straight, dragging MacDowall up by the lapels to keep their faces level. MacDowall was now blubbering freely.

'Well, what's it like to be bullied? You don't like it much, do you?'

He dropped MacDowall and pushed him hard against the tin.

'And you'll like it even less if I ever catch you at it again.'

He enunciated this warning slowly and carefully, as though MacDowall was a foreigner, having difficulty with the language.

'UNDERSTAND?'

'Yes, Sir.'

'Good. Now get into school, get cleaned up and . . . wait a minute, I've got your form next, haven't I?'

'Yes, Sir.'

'Right then, you can spend it shovelling that lot back into shape.'

He pivoted on his left foot and toe-ended a lump of coke back across the asphalt. It cannoned into other lumps, then took its place amongst the spread. A glance away and it was lost.

'And when I come out at twelve o'clock I want every lump back in its place. Right?'

'Yes, Sir.'

'Right. Get cracking.'

MacDowall walked away, rubbing his eyes and his cheeks with his knuckles and the backs of his hands. He stopped rubbing them to glance at Billy as he passed. Mr Farthing followed him slowly out of the shed, timing his confrontation with Billy to coincide with the disappearance of MacDowall round the corner of the building.

'Now then, Casper, what's it all about?'

Billy shook his head.

'What do you mean?' . . . Mr Farthing mimicked him. 'It must have been something.'

'O . . . I can't tell you right, Sir.'

'Why can't you?'

''Cos I can't. I can't, Sir!'

The skin on his face tightened, pulling at his mouth and his eyes, and he began to cry again.

'He started calling me names an' sayin' things about my dad an' my mother an' our Jud, an' everybody wa' laughin', an' . . .'

His sobs became so violent that they impaired his breathing and interrupted his speech. Mr Farthing held up one hand, nodding.

'All right, lad, calm down. It's finished with now.'

He waited for him to calm down, then shook his head slowly.

'I don't know, you always seem to cop it, don't you, Casper?'

Billy stood with his head bowed, sniffing quietly to himself.

'I wonder why? Why do you think it is?'

'What, Sir?'

'That you're always in trouble?'

''Cos everybody picks on me, that's why.'

He looked up with such intensity that his eyes and the tears webbed in the lower lashes seemed to fuse and shine like lumps of crystal. Mr Farthing looked away to hide a smile.

'Yes I know they do, but why?'

'I don't know, they just do, that's all.'

'Perhaps it's because you're a bad lad.'

'P'raps I am, sometimes. But I'm not that bad, I'm no worse than stacks o' kids, but they just seem to get away with it.'

from *A Kestrel for a Knave* by Barry Hines

* Do you think Mr Farthing does the right thing?
Discuss which of these alternatives below would have been best once he had stopped the fight, 1. for MacDowall, 2. for Billy Casper. He should

> a. send him to the headmaster (who will probably cane him)
> b. see the boy's form teacher or year tutor and ask for a report on his general attitude and behaviour before taking any further action
> c. give him a stiff lecture and leave it at that
> d. make him spend his breaks in detention for a time
> e. give him a physical shaking-up and leave it at that
> f. get in touch with the boy's parents to tell them what is going on and ask for their help
> g. do nothing
> h. try to find out why the boy has got into the fight and offer him sympathy or advice.

If you have suggested **different** courses of action for MacDowall and Casper, can you justify treating them differently?

* Look at what Mr Farthing does to MacDowall. Is Mr Farthing a bully?

* 'You always seem to cop it, don't you, Casper? . . . Perhaps it's because you're a bad lad.'
'P'raps I am, sometimes. But I'm not that bad, I'm no worse than stacks o' kids, but they just seem to get away with it.'
Why do some people always seem to get into trouble while others escape? Or does it only look that way to people who are often in trouble?

1. As headmaster of a school you have to write a booklet of advice to be given to teachers starting their first jobs. Write the article you would include on 'How to deal with bullying'.

Incident

You are walking along a school corridor. In the cloakroom a girl is intimidating a much younger boy who is obviously about to start crying. Some of the girl's friends are egging her on. Two friends of the boy are standing back, looking worried. You see the boy have his arm twisted, and hand over a coin to the girl. You recognise the girl, who has a reputation for intimidating others.
What would you do?

Here are some **possible** courses of action to discuss with others in the class:

1. Ignore it. 2. Fetch a teacher. 3. Tell the girls to stop. 4. Wait until the girls have gone and then comfort the boy. 5. Tell the boy's form teacher or year tutor.	6. Tell the girl's form teacher or year tutor. 7. Get some of your friends to help 'sort out' the girls. 8. Tell the headteacher. 9. Threaten the girls that you will tell unless they stop. 10. Try to stop the girls physically.

Working with someone else, each suppose you are either:

A teacher in his or her first year, or
The deputy headmaster or headmistress.

What would you do as these people?
Here are some possible courses of action to discuss:

1. Ignore it. 2. Tell them to stop and do nothing further if they obey. 3. Move them all out of the cloakrooms and leave it at that. 4. Tell them to move on or stop but don't wait to see if they obey. 5. Find out their names and report the incident to the appropriate form teachers or year tutors.	6. Take the girls to the headteacher. 7. Take them all to the headteacher. 8. Go and seek immediate help from another member of staff.

After **immediate** action what would you do? What do you think of these suggestions:

> talk to the boy and girl together
> talk to them separately
> give the girl 'Some of her own medicine'
> sympathise with the boy
> tell the boy he should not be so weak
> tell the girl that she is behaving childishly
> send the girl home with a letter to her parents?

Choose your Victim Carefully

Attempts at bullying can have their funnier side . . .
Benjamin 'Mouse' Fawley has annoyed an older and much bigger boy, Mark
Hammerman, and is expecting Hammerman to beat him up. Mouse is talking
things over with a friend, Ezzie.

'You ever been hit before, Mouse? I mean, hard?' Ezzie asked.

Mouse sighed. The conversation had now passed beyond the question of whether Hammerman would attack. It was now a question of whether he, Mouse Fawley, could survive the attack. He said thickly, remembering, 'Four times.'

'Four times in one fight? I mean, you stood up for four hits, Mouse?' There was grudging admiration in his voice.

Mouse shook his head. 'Four hits – four fights.'

'You went right down each time? I mean POW and you went down, POW and you went down, POW and you went –'

'Yes!'

'Where did you take these hits?' Ezzie asked, straightening suddenly. Ezzie had never taken a single direct blow in his life because he was a good dodger. Sometimes his mother chased him through the apartment, striking at him while he dodged and ducked, crying, 'Look out, Mom, look out now! You're going to hit me!'

He asked again, 'Where were you hit?'

Mouse said, 'In the stomach.'

'All four times?'

'Yeah.' Mouse suddenly thought of his stomach as having a big red circular target on it with HIT HERE printed in the centre.

'Who hit you?'

'Two boys in Cincinnati when I was on vacation, and a boy named Mickey Swearinger, and somebody else I don't remember.' He lowered his head because he remembered the fourth person all right, but he didn't want to tell Ezzie about it. If he had added the name of Viola Angotti to the list of those who had hit him in the stomach, Ezzie's face would have screwed up with laughter. 'Viola Angotti hit you? No fooling, Viola Angotti?' It was the sort of thing Ezzie could carry on about for hours. 'Viola Angotti. *The* Viola Angotti?'

And Mouse would have had to keep sitting there saying over and over, 'Yes, Viola Angotti hit me in the stomach. Yes, *the* Viola Angotti.' And then he would have to tell Ezzie all about it, every detail, how one recess long ago the boys had decided to put some girls in the school trash cans. It had been one of those suggestions that stuns everyone with its rightness. Some one had said, 'Hey, let's put those girls over there in the trash cans!'

and the plan won immediate acceptance. Nothing could have been more appropriate. The trash cans were big and had just been emptied, and in an instant the boys were off chasing the girls and yelling at the tops of their lungs.

It had been wonderful at first, Mouse remembered. Primitive blood had raced through his body. The desire to capture had driven him like a wild man through the school yard, up the sidewalk, everywhere. He understood what had driven the cave man and the barbarian, because this same passion was driving him. Putting the girls in the trash cans was the most important challenge of his life. His long screaming charge ended with him red-faced, gasping for breath – and with Viola Angotti pinned against the garbage cans.

His moment of triumph was short. It lasted about two seconds. Then it began to dim as he realized, first, that it *was* Viola Angotti, and, second, that he was not going to be able to get her into the garbage can without a great deal of help.

He cried, 'Hey, you guys, come on, I've got one,' but behind him the school yard was silent. Where was everybody? he had wondered uneasily. As it turned out, the principal had caught the other boys, and they were all being marched back in the front door of the school, but Mouse didn't know this.

He called again, 'Come on, you guys, get the lid off this garbage can, will you?'

And then, when he said that, Viola Angotti had taken two steps forward. She said, 'Nobody's putting *me* in no garbage can.' He could still remember how she had looked standing there. She had recently taken the part of the Statue of Liberty in a class play, and somehow she seemed taller and stronger at this moment than when she had been in costume.

He cried, 'Hey, you guys!' It was a plea. 'Where are you?'

And then Viola Angotti had taken one more step, and with a faint sigh she had socked him in the stomach so hard that he had doubled over and lost his lunch. He hadn't known it was possible to be hit like that outside a boxing ring. It was the hardest blow he had ever taken. Viola Angotti could be heavyweight champion of the world.

As she walked past his crumpled body she had said again, 'Nobody's putting me in no garbage can.' It had sounded like one of the world's basic truths. The sun will rise. The tides will flow. Nobody's putting Viola Angotti in no garbage can.

Later, when he thought about it, he realized that he had been lucky. If she had wanted to, Viola Angotti could have capped her victory by tossing his rag-doll body into the garbage can and slamming down the lid. Then, when the principal came out on to the playground calling, 'Benjamin Fawley! Has anybody seen Benjamin Fawley?' he would have had to moan. 'I'm in here.' He would have had to climb out of the garbage can in front of the whole school. His shame would have followed him for life. When he was a grown man, people would still be pointing him out to their children. '*That*'s the man that Viola Angotti stuffed into the garbage can.'

from *The Eighteenth Emergency* by Betsy Byars

1. Understandably, Mouse keeps to himself the story of his humiliating defeat by Viola Angotti. Think about a time when **you** were made to feel small or embarrassed, but which now, as an older person, you find funny. Write the story of what happened, trying to share the funny side of it with your readers.

2. Write a story about someone who dreams of being really strong and successful but is brought down to earth with a bump when he or she tries to act out those dreams.

The Victim

They were packing their schoolbags to go home. Across the classroom, alone as always, Nicky was packing his neat books, expensive drawing instruments into an expensive bag, nearly new. But all scuffed, mauled.

Nicky's time of ordeal had come. He looked pale, was already starting to pant. Outside, the wolf-pack was gathering: waiting to pull his bag from his hand, strew his books over the pavement, kick him when he bent down to pick them up, pour gravel down his shirt, pull his shoes off and throw them over walls. Not till Nicky was reduced to screaming blind hysterics would he be allowed to creep home weeping.

Every night it happened, regular as clockwork. The wolf-pack never tired of it. Mornings, they didn't bother. They were sleepy or had homework worries, or were late. But the end of the day was always rounded off by an hour of torture.

Chas looked at Nicky. The face was good-looking, with a pale girl's good looks. The hair was curly and kept long. He had an operation scar on the side of his neck. But did that explain the constant bullying? Every kid had *some* peculiarity – was fat or thin or had big ears. Chas got twitted because he had thick lips and a funny fold of skin on the back of his neck. So why was Nicky singled out?

Chas wondered how he himself felt about Nicky. He'd never touched him, but constantly teased him. Why? Chas shrugged.

* Why does the writer make a point of telling us that Nicky's belongings were, 'neat . . . expensive . . . nearly new'?

* Why is the gang which chases Nicky called 'the wolf-pack'?

* Why does the gang let Nicky go once he becomes hysterical and starts crying?

* 'So why was Nicky singled out?'
What do you think makes people the target of bullying?
    Is it because of their physical build or appearance?
    Is it because of their personality?
    Is it because of the way they react to being teased?
    Is it because of their background, their home circumstances?
    Or is it none or all of these? Are there other reasons?

* Look at the description of what the 'wolf-pack' does to Nicky every night and how he reacts. Why don't they get tired of it? Why do they enjoy it?

* What advice or comfort could you offer to Nicky?

Nicky later gets support from some of his classmates. Chas McGill, Clogger and Seb walk home with Nicky to protect him from the gang of bullies led by Boddser Brown.

Boddser stepped out in front.

'Right, McGill, you've asked for this.' His bluster was gone. He had made up his mind, as a man might decide to nail up a fence he'd watched sagging all winter. Chas had made Boddser's dignity sag a bit lately; now it was to be mended with Chas's blood. Boddser didn't even sound cruel or gloating as he did when he tortured Nicky; just determined. The time for talk, Chas decided, was over. It was time for action. But what? Chas was quick, and not soft, but no one he knew could stand up for long to the pounding of Boddser's fists, except perhaps Clogger, and it wasn't Clogger's fight.

He could dive, head down, for Boddser's midriff, slide down and pinion Boddser's legs and hope to push him over. But that would end, inevitably, with Boddser sitting on his chest, banging his head against the pavement.

Boddser took off his gasmask haversack, then his school-bag, his school raincoat, his blazer. He rolled up his sleeves slowly, one after the other. Chas could think of nothing but to do likewise. He took off his gasmask case. It was not like Boddser's. It was a circular tin, twice the size of a large tin of beans and nearly as heavy. It swung from a long thin leather strap.

And then the idea came to Charles. It set him aghast. But it was maim or be maimed now. He put the case down carefully and took off his schoolbag and coat and blazer, laying them in the fine gravel of the gutter. He came up with his fists clenched, ready. Boddser advanced without hurry.

'Take your specs off,' shouted Chas. 'I don't want your Mum complaining to me dad if I break them!'

'Playing for time, McGill,' jeered Boddser. 'That won't save you.' But he took off his spectacles and handed them to a minion, and advanced again. Chas saw the first blow coming, and ducked it.

Then he swung his right fist wildly, a yard from Boddser's face, and opened his hand. Fine gravel sprayed into Boddser's eyes. There was no need for the second handful. The huge menacing figure was suddenly crouched up helpless, tears streaming down his face.

Calmly, full of murder, Chas picked up his gasmask case and swung it. It hit the side of Boddser's head with a sound like a splitting pumpkin. Boddser screamed but did not fall. Chas swung at him again. The gasmask case dented dramatically. Boddser crashed into the corrugated-iron fence. Chas raised his tin a third time. All the hate of all the years, infant school, junior school, boiled up in him.

It was as well that Cem snatched the gasmask from his hand.

'You're bloody mad. Stop it, stop it!' Cem yelled. Chas snatched for his weapon again. Clogger kicked it away and held Chas's arms behind his back. Then everyone watched Boddser aghast as he reeled about, blood spurting from both hands held across his face. . . .

. . . It was Clogger who approached the moaning lump, pulled the hands away and looked. . . .

. . . 'Shut your wailing man; ye'll live,' he said to Boddser. 'Stop going on like a wee bairn.' He turned to the group. 'We'd better be getting him to the hospital.'

Fortunately it was only two hundred yards away. A stiff starched sister took over.

'How did this happen?' she said like a High Court judge.

'I hit him,' said Chas.

'What with?'

'Me gasmask.'

'You're a wicked, vicious boy,' said the sister. 'I shall ring up your headmaster personally. You grammar-school boys should know better. You might have killed him.'

'He was bigger than me!'

'That's no excuse. British boys fight with their fists!' Chas felt like a criminal.

'British boys fight with their fists,' said Chas's dad, and went off to mend the greenhouse. He didn't speak to Chas for two whole days, and neither did his mother, even all through the air-raids.

'Britishers do not use weapons, they fight only with their fists,' said the headmaster, flexing his cane. 'Bend over boy!' It was six of the best and very painful.

The class treated him with awe-struck and horrified silence. It was their opinion that Boddser had asked for it, but Chas shouldn't have done it.

'But what do you *do* if you're small?' asked Chas hopelessly. Nobody answered; they got on with their classwork.

from *The Machine-Gunners* by Robert Westall

* Think about the way these people reacted to what Chas did:

   the nursing sister
   Chas's parents
   Chas's headmaster
   Chas's classmates.

Are they right to react as they do? Are they fair? Does Chas deserve his punishments?
Discuss your ideas with others in the class.

* How do you think *you* would react to this incident if you were:

  a friend of Chas
  one of his neighbours
  one of his parents
  the headteacher at his school
  one of Boddser's parents?

* 'Calmly, full of murder, Chas picked up his gasmask case and swung it' . . .
'It was as well that Cem snatched the gasmask from his hand.'

Discuss these questions about Chas:

  Does Chas enjoy hitting Boddser?
  Is he out of control?
  Is he mad, as Cem says?
  Is he vicious?
  Is he dangerous?
  Is he a criminal?

* 'But what **do** you do if you're small?'
How would *you* answer that question?

* Do you feel any sympathy for Boddser?

1. If the police had been called, Chas would probably have ended up in court. Write the statement he might have made in his defence.

2. Improvise or write the scenes at school in which the headmaster interviews the parents of Boddser and Chas.

3. Write or improvise the conversations at home which might follow these interviews at school.

Dear Mary Allinson

Suppose you run an advice column in a weekly magazine and you receive this letter:

> 42, Briars Avenue,
> Kidderminster,
> Worcestershire.
>
> Dear Mary Allinson,
>
> Will you help me please? I am 13 and go to a comprehensive school and I am being bullied every day. I am scared to go home after school because they always get me, and if I don't give them money then they always punch me and tear up my books. I wanted to tell my year tutor but I don't believe in telling and anyway if I did that they would know and only make it worse for me.
>
> I asked my mother and she said I would have to fight my own battles.
>
> I think if I don't get an answer soon I will have to leave home. My dad left home about a year ago, or I could maybe ask him.
>
> Please write back.
>
> K. L. Noble.

All serious letters of this sort are replied to, whether or not they are published in the magazine.

If you were 'Mary Allinson' (this is often a fictitious name: 'she' may be a man), how would you reply?

K. L. Noble gives only limited information: we do not know if it is a boy or girl; we do not know **why** he or she has become the victim of bullying; we do not know who 'they' are – whether they are boys or girls, or their ages.

Before you reply to the letter, you must think carefully about **all** the problems faced by K. L. Noble, and consider all possible solutions to them. Try to identify each problem and weigh up how important it is. The questions and suggestions below may help you to work out your reply:

1. K. L. Noble has already considered some possible steps to take: should you suggest that he or she look at these again more carefully?

2. K. L. Noble has already been given some advice: should he or she be persuaded to think about that advice again, or is that advice not very helpful in this case?

3. There is a note of desperation in the letter: can you offer some **comfort** as well as advice?

4. Should your reply try to make K. L. Noble look carefully at himself or herself to try to discover some of the **reasons** for the bullying?

5. You should try to offer **two** kinds of help in your letter:
   a. help to relieve his or her immediate suffering
   b. advice which may help K. L. Noble to prevent this sort of thing happening again in the future.

Friedrich

This extract from Friedrich *is set in Germany in 1938. During that year Nazis organised attacks against Jews throughout the country. The storyteller, who is thirteen, has a Jewish friend of the same age, called Friedrich Schneider. Friedrich lives with his parents in the flat above his. On his way home from school one day the storyteller sees a crowd of people breaking into a Jewish home for apprentices.*

'Open up!' he shouted to the upper floors of the home.

But nothing stirred, no window opened, not even a curtain moved. The house seemed dead.

The man bawled his order a second time to shut windows.

Our eyes were all glued to the building. I was very excited. What would happen?

Nothing did!

One of the women reviled the Jewish home in an ugly voice.

I couldn't understand what she said because her voice was so shrill.

10   The man paid no attention to the screeching. With heavy steps he marched towards the heavy oak door. He pressed down the handle, but the door was locked.

He stepped back three, four steps, and threw his back against the door. He tried again, this time taking a longer run.

Again nothing!

Other men from the group joined in. At first singly, then in unison, they threw themselves against the door of the building.

Even the women leaped to their aid.

Only the woman who had been so abusive earlier stayed where she was;
20   she cheered the others on.

Soon her 'one – two – three – one – two – three!' resounded through the street.

And in the rhythm of her shouts, men and women hurled themselves against the door.

From the circle of bystanders more and more joined in. Egged on by the woman, they gradually joined her chant. It was then that I caught myself shouting 'one – two – three' and edging closer with each shout. All at once I, too, was straining at the door and didn't know how I had got there. I also noticed that no one was watching now.

30   All took part.

Very slowly the door gave way. When it finally burst open, no one expected it. Those in the first row fell into the house. The ones behind them stumbled across the wreckage. The rest crowded in after.

I was pulled along with the throng. When I had a chance to stop and look around me, the sounds of crashing and bumping came from all parts of the house.

As I climbed the stairs with my schoolbag, bedside tables zoomed by and burst apart at the bottom of the stairs.

All this was strangely exhilarating.

40 No one stopped the destruction. Of the people living in the house, none were to be seen. Nothing but empty corridors, empty rooms.

In one of the bedrooms I came across the woman who had done the shouting. She was slashing open mattresses with a vegetable knife. She smiled at me in a cloud of dust. 'Don't you know me any more?' she asked in a squeaky voice.

I thought, then shook my head.

She laughed out loud. 'When I bring you your paper every morning?' With the back of her hand, she wiped her mouth, lifted a bottle of milk to her lips and drank from it. Then she put the bottle down again and whirled
50 the slashed mattress out of the window.

A middle-aged man had come across a tool box. He was stuffing all his pockets, and he pressed a brand new hammer into my hand.

At first I just played with the hammer. Without paying attention I swung it loosely from my wrist, back and forth, back and forth. At one point I must have nicked something – glass crashed at my blow.

I jumped. The glass had belonged to a bookcase. But almost at once my curiosity awoke. Gently I tapped a cracked pane of glass and it fell out of its frame. By now I was enjoying myself. I swung so hard against the third pane that its splinters fell in bursts to the floor.

60 With my hammer I cut myself a path through the corridors, smashing aside whatever barred my way: legs of chairs, toppled wardrobes, chamber pots and glassware. I felt so strong! I could have sung I was so drunk with the desire to swing my hammer.

I discovered a door leading to a small classroom that hadn't been touched yet. Curiously, I looked around.

Turning, I hit against a T-square with my schoolbag. It clattered to the floor and I stepped on it by mistake. It burst with a loud bang that sounded like a shot.

I stopped short. Lots more T-squares hung on the wall. I took down
70 another and repeated the bang. This time, the sound was deeper. One after the other, I bent T-squares till they broke. And I enjoyed the fact that each had a different tone to it.

When I couldn't find any more T-squares, I picked up my hammer from the podium. I drummed it along the desk tops and searched all the cupboards and desk drawers in the room. But I found nothing else to satisfy my lust for destruction.

Disappointed, I was about to leave the room, but by the door I looked back one last time. Against the far wall stood a large blackboard. I pulled back my arm and hurled the hammer. It struck the centre of the

80   blackboard. The head remained stuck. The light handle projected from the black surface. All of a sudden I felt tired and disgusted. On the stairs, I found half a mirror. I looked in it. Then I ran home.

Mother was already waiting for me. She looked at me, but said nothing. I didn't tell her where I had been.

Mother served the soup. I began to eat.

At that moment, we heard yells outside our house.

The front door was pushed open, accompanied by shouts.

Herr Resch complained loudly.

Noisily many people clattered up the stairs, past our door and higher.

90   The Schneiders' door burst open with a bang.

'What's that?' Mother asked, pale and horrified.

We heard a cry – Frau Schneider!

'We must call the police!'

Something fell to the floor with a muffled sound.

'The police don't do anything,' I replied. 'They watch.'

A man's voice swore.

Friedrich cried out, then howled hopelessly.

I threw down my spoon and ran to the door.

'Stay here!' Mother wailed.

100   I raced up the stairs.

The Schneiders' door dangled from a hinge. The glass had splintered from its frame.

In the kitchen Frau Schneider lay on the floor, her lips blue, her breathing laboured.

Friedrich had a lump the size of a fist on his forehead. He bent over his mother, talking to her in a whisper. He didn't notice me.

A man stepped across Frau Schneider's legs without looking down. He emptied a large box of silver cutlery out of the window.

In the living room a woman was smashing china plates. 'Meissen!' she said proudly, when she noticed me.

110   Another woman was slashing every picture in the room with Herr Schneider's letter opener.

A dark-haired giant stood by Herr Schneider's bookcase. He took one volume after another from the shelves. He gripped each book by its binding and tore it apart in the middle. 'Bet you can't do the same!' he boasted with a laugh.

In Friedrich's room a man was trying to push the whole bedframe through the window. 'Come and help!' he invited me.

I slunk downstairs again.

120   Mother was peering through a crack in the door, trembling. Fearfully, she pulled me into the flat. She pushed me into our living room.

We stood by the window and looked down on the street. Above us the crashing and tramping continued.

'Jew, kick the bucket!' a woman screeched outside. It was our newspaper lady.

An armchair rushed past our window and thudded into the rosebushes in our front garden.

Mother began to weep loudly.

I wept with her.

from *Friedrich* by Hans Peter Richter

* How does the storyteller become involved in the attack on the home for apprentices? Does he want to join in? Does he understand why he has become involved?

* 'I felt so strong! I could have sung I was so drunk with the desire to swing my hammer.' (lines 62 to 63) How does this help to explain why the crowd is involved in such senseless vandalism?

* 'All of a sudden I felt tired and disgusted.' (line 81) What has made the storyteller feel this?

* 'I found half a mirror. I looked in it. Then I ran home.' (lines 81 to 82) Why does he mention the mirror, do you think?

* Why does the storyteller twice mention the fact that one of the people who is most active in the destruction is the woman who delivers their newspapers?

* 'A man stepped across Frau Schneider's legs without looking down.' (line 107) What does this tell you about the man's state of mind and about what is happening to the people in the mob?

* In the house for apprentices a man gave the storyteller a hammer which the storyteller used to help break up the home; in the Schneider's flat a man who is breaking up the furniture says, 'Come and help!' but the storyteller does not. Why has his attitude changed?

* What are your feelings about the part the storyteller's mother plays in these events?

* 'The police don't do anything. They watch.' (line 95) What does this tell you about the society they are living in in Germany in 1938?

1. Write an essay in which you try to answer some of the questions below. It may help you to organise your writing if you use a separate paragraph to discuss each question or each group of linked questions.

> Is it right to call the persecution of the Jews in Germany in the 1930s and early 1940s *bullying*? Does the kind of incident described here have anything in common with bullying by children or teenagers? Are there any important differences?

Do adults bully one another as much as children do?

Why are old and frail people often the victims of young attackers?

Do adults bully children?

Some people enjoy bullying others — it makes them feel strong. Can these feelings be exploited by governments, by political parties, or by other organised groups?

Are wars ever cases of bullying on a large scale or is that explanation too simple?

2. Write a story about someone who gets involved in bullying and later regrets what he or she has done.

A Closer Look

1. 'I couldn't understand what she said because her voice was so shrill.' (line 9) Why does the writer include this detail, do you think? What does it tell us about the woman's state of mind?

2. How does the writer emphasise the stillness and emptiness of the home for apprentices in the first fifty lines of this extract?

3. The storyteller says, **'By now I was enjoying myself.'** (line 58) What else does he say that shows that he enjoys breaking up the home for apprentices?

4. **'Friedrich had a lump the size of a fist on his forehead.'** (line 105) Why is this a very effective way of describing Friedrich's injury?

5. The writer places some very short sentences in paragraphs on their own:
    'All took part.' (line 30)
    'All this was strangely exhilarating.' (line 39)
    'I slunk downstairs again.' (line 119)
    'I wept with her.' (line 129)
Why does the writer do this?

6. The writer is describing very violent events here, but he writes in a rather 'dead pan' style: that is, he writes in a flat, unemotional way. What effect does this style of writing have on your feelings about the events he describes?

Lescale's Automatic Fire Escape

spring

ratchet

LESCALE'S AUTOMATIC FIRE ESCAPE

The modern multi-storey buildings with their frequently narrow passageways and exits should be equipped with an appropriate means of rapid escape for the occupants in case of fire. Mr John M. Lescale has now devised a life-saving appliance on wheels, which may be kept in the house as a piece of furniture, to be moved to a balcony or window in the event of fire breaking out.

After folding out the brackets of the apparatus, the person wishing to escape takes his seat in one of the loops formed by a length of cable with a ring and a hook, and attached to a cable (A or B) which is wound onto a reel. (C) While descending, the user grips the rope (D) connected to the braking device (E) with one hand. Only when this rope is pulled can the cable uncoil from the reel to permit descent. When the descent is completed another person may leave the building by using the second cable, during which operation the first cable is automatically pulled up. In this way, a large number of people can leave the burning building.

∗ With a partner, check how the machine is supposed to work, stage by stage. Would this fire escape work, or is it a useless invention? Discuss your ideas and theories with others in the class.

1. Write a report on the fire escape for a committee which is considering installing it in a block of flats. Include a report of tests on the machine and explain its disadvantages and any advantages you can find. End your report by recommending that the committee should go ahead with its plans or abandon them.

2. Try to design an alternative fire escape for use in high buildings. The device might be entirely your own invention or it could be a much modified version of Mr Lescale's. Design and write a short leaflet to advertise your invention. Your design should consider the following points:

   the fire escape should allow a large number of people to leave the building in safety
   it should not be too expensive
   it should not be dangerous when not in use
   old people and young children should be able to use it without assistance
   it should not be too bulky or unsightly.

Spelling

Revision

deceive
receive
conceive
perceive

seize
weird

diagram
diagonal
diamond
dialect

courageous
outrageous
miscellaneous

rhyme
rhythm

prominent
imminent

centre
metre
theatre

attached
detached

gradient
obedient

loneliness
business

approximately
immediately

rarely
sincerely

accidentally
basically
frantically
sarcastically
automatically

beautiful   beautifully
faithful   faithfully

saviour
behaviour

irregular
irresistible
irresponsible

resident
independent

different
opponent

*   *   *

advertise
advertisement

loose
noose
goose

privilege
college
allege

ferocious
vicious

hyphen
hygiene
hyacinth
hysteria
hypocrite

necessary
accession
recession

fiction
faction
dictionary

interrupt
interrogate
interrelated

sealed
revealed
annealed

government
environment

pneumatic
pneumonia

aspire
aspirate
aspirin

school
scholar
scheme
schedule

noticeable
manageable
agreeable
knowledgeable

municipal
principal

dissatisfied
dissimilar
dissuade
dissolve
dissemble
dissent
disseminate

acquired
acquitted
acquaintance

ceremony
cereal
cerebral

accent
access
accept
accede
accelerate
success

disciple
discipline

psalm
pseudo-
psychic
psychiatrist
psoriasis

immediate
imminent
immerse
immure
immense
immortal

called
enthralled
appalled

hymn
autumn
column
solemn
condemn
damnation
mnemonic

benediction
beneficial
benefited

blurred
furred
purred

aquarium
aqualung
aquatic

aggravated
aggression
aggrieved

primeval
coeval
medieval

phrase
phantom
phenomenon

luncheon
truncheon

vigorous
rigorous
humorous

architect
architrave
archipelago
archbishop

judicial
judicious
prejudice

emission
omission
permission
remission
commission

preferred
deferred
interred
deterred
occurred

corrected
corrupted
corroded
corrugated

skilful
fulfil

accommodation
commodore
common

stationer
stationery

symmetry
symmetrical
sympathy
sympathetic
symphony

Index to Language Topics

The authors and publishers wish to thank the following copyright owners for permission to quote from copyright works.

Page 7 from *Prove Yourself a Hero* © K. M. Peyton 1977, by permission of Oxford University Press; page 11 adapted from *Phobias and Obsessions* by Joy Melville, George Allen and Unwin (Publishers) Ltd; page 13 from *This was the Old Chief's Country*. Copyright 1951 Doris Lessing. Reprinted by permission of Curtis Brown Ltd, London, on behalf of Doris Lessing; page 15 from *The Tower* by Marghanita Laski, Hamish Hamilton Children's Books Ltd; page 22 'Poem' by Hugh Sykes Davies from *Poetry of the 30's*, Penguin Books Ltd; page 28 from *Earth Is Room Enough* by Isaac Asimov, Granada Publishing Ltd; page 33 from *What About It, Sharon?* by John Harvey, Peacock Books; page 43 from *The Rainbow* by D. H. Lawrence, William Heinemann Ltd and Penguin Books Ltd. By permission of Laurence Pollinger Ltd and the Estate of Frieda Lawrence Ravagli; page 47 from 'The Observer' 10 October 1982, by Auriol Stevens; page 72 'The Unseen Housemate' by Wilfrid Gibson from *The*

Albemarle Book of Verse for Schools. By permission of Macmillan, London and Basingstoke; page 74 from *A Night at a Cottage* by Richard Hughes, Chatto and Windus Ltd; page 80 from 'The Guardian' 19 March 1982; pages 84–5 adapted from 'The Guardian' 15, 17, 22 August 1981; page 86 from *Journey from Obscurity* by Harold Owen, abridged and edited by H. M. Gornall, © Oxford University Press 1968. Reprinted by permission of Oxford University Press; page 88 'Millers End' from *Collected Poems* by Charles Causley, Macmillan London and Basingstoke; page 93 from *Ishi in Two Worlds* by Theodora Kroeber, University of California Press; page 98 'Snake' from *The Complete Poems of D. H. Lawrence*, William Heinemann Ltd. By permission of Laurence Pollinger Ltd and the Estate of Frieda Lawrence Ravagli; page 103 'Car Fights Cat' by Alan Sillitoe from *Here Today* edited by Ted Hughes, Hutchinson Publishing Group Ltd; page 104 reprinted by permission of Faber and Faber Ltd from *The Inheritors* by William Golding; page 106 from *The War of the Worlds* by H. G. Wells. By permission of the Executors of the estate of the late H. G. Wells and William Heinemann Ltd; page 111 'Southbound on the Freeway' from *New and Selected Things Taking Place* by May Swenson. Copyright © 1963 by May Swenson. First appeared in *The New Yorker*. By permission of Little, Brown and Company in association with the Atlantic Monthly Press; page 119 'The Lesson' from *A Tropical Childhood and Other Poems* by Edward Lucie-Smith, © Oxford University Press 1961. Reprinted by permission of Oxford University Press; page 120 from *A Waltz through the Hills* by G. M. Glaskin, Barrie and Rockliffe; page 123 from *Two Lamps in our Street* by Arthur Barton, Hutchinson Publishing Group Ltd; page 127 from *A High Wind in Jamaica* by Richard Hughes, Chatto and Windus; page 131 reprinted by permission of Faber and Faber Ltd from *Christopher Columbus* by Louis MacNeice; pages 147–8 (1) from *The Young Unicorns* by Madeleine L'Engle, Puffin; (2) from *An Only Child* by Frank O'Connor. Reprinted by permission of A. D. Peters and Co Ltd; (3) from *The Oceans* by David Lambert, Ward Lock Educational Ltd; (4) from *The Caterpillar's Story* by Katrin Brandt, Puffin; (5) from *Great Sea Mysteries* by Richard Garrett, Pan; page 164 from *Olga* by Justin Beecham, Paddington Press Ltd; page 166 from *The Barry John Story* by Barry John, Collins Publishers; pages 169, 170 from *Born Under a Bad Sign* by Tony Palmer, William Kimber and Co Ltd; page 173 from *Double Bill* by Alec McCowen, Elm Tree Books; page 176 from *Cider With Rosie* by Laurie Lee, The Hogarth Press Ltd; page 186 from *The Desperadoes and Other Stories* by Stan Barstow, Michael Joseph Ltd; page 193 from *The Friends* by Rosa Guy, Victor Gollancz Ltd; page 196 from *Kestral for a Knave* by Barry Hines, Michael Joseph Ltd; page 203, the extract from *The Eighteenth Emergency* by Betsy Byars is reproduced by permission of The Bodley Head; page 206 from *The Machine Gunners* by Robert Westall, Macmillan London and Basingstoke; page 212 from *Friedrich* by Hans Peter Richter, trans. Edite Kroll (Kestrel Books 1975). Copyright © 1961 by Sebaldus-Verlag G.m.b.H. Nurnberg; © 1970 by Holt, Rinehart and Winston Inc. Reprinted by permission of Penguin Books Ltd; page 218 from *Victorian Inventions* compiled by Leonard de Vries in collaboration with Ilonka van Amstel, published by John Murray.